DESCENDING
LIKE A DOVE

D1016206

Descending Like a Dove

CLIVE CALVER

Charisma
HOUSE
A STRANG COMPANY

Most STRANG COMMUNICATIONS/CHARISMA HOUSE/SILOAM products are available at special quantity discounts for bulk purchase for sales promotions, premiums, fund-raising and educational needs. For details, write Strang Communications/Charisma House/Siloam, 600 Rinehart Road, Lake Mary, Florida 32746, or telephone (407) 333−0600.

DESCENDING LIKE A DOVE by Clive Calver
Published by Charisma House
A Strang Company
600 Rinehart Road
Lake Mary, Florida 32746
www.charismahouse.com

Unless otherwise noted, all Scripture quotations are from the Holy Bible, New International Version. Copyright © 1973, 1978, 1984, International Bible Society. Used by permission.

Scripture quotations marked GNT are from the Good News Translation, Second Edition, copyright © 1992 by American Bible Society. Used by permission.

Scripture quotations marked KJV are from the King James Version of the Bible.

Scripture quotations marked NKJV are from the New King James Version of the Bible. Copyright © 1979, 1980, 1982 by Thomas Nelson, Inc., publishers. Used by permission.

Scripture quotations marked PHILLIPS are from *The New Testament in Modern English*, Revised Edition. Copyright © 1958, 1960, 1972 by J. B. Phillips. Macmillan Publishing Co. Used by permission.

Cover design by Ededron J. Hernandez

Library of Congress Cataloging-in-Publication Data

Calver, Clive.
  Descending like a dove / Clive Calver.
    p. cm.
Includes bibliographical references.
  ISBN 1-59185-290-0 (pbk.)
  1. Holy Spirit. I. Title.
BT121.3.C35 2004
231'.3—dc22
                                  2003022744

This book was previously published as *The Holy Spirit* by Scripture Union, 207−209 Queensway, Bletchley, MK2 2EB, England, ISBN 1-85999-527-6, copyright © 1984, 2001.

04 05 06 07 — 987654321
Printed in the United States of America

To Graham Kendrick, worship leader, hymn writer, and long-time partner in ministry during the years in Britain. Without his friendship and support throughout the early years, much of this book could never have been written, and without it now, some of the rest would not be taking place.

Acknowledgments

No book can ever be a completely solo project. Many people are involved at various stages, and they should all receive their fair share of the credit. The blame I reserve for myself!

To complicate the situation further, many years have passed between the first and second editions of this book in Britain, and now this new edition in the U.S. Despite living in the States for the last six years, I still have a long way to go before I have assimilated all those cultural and linguistic differences that combine to make us what that famous Irish dramatist and socialist George Bernard Shaw described as "two peoples separated by a common language." So my grateful thanks go to all who feature in these pages or who have contributed toward their production—both in Britain and America.

I do want to thank Stephen Strang, who has been a trusted friend over the years, and all the staff of Strang Communications for believing that this book really does have a message today for the church in the United States. My sincere appreciation goes especially to those who translated my "English" and who worked to make this manuscript more relevant to America.

I am indebted to Scripture Union for their original invitation to write this book in both its first and second editions. I also want to thank them for permission to publish this manuscript in the U.S. In the same way, I am grateful to everyone who has supported and encouraged its publication on each side of the Atlantic.

My thanks are also due to the Board of World Relief and to my colleagues for offering their support and allowing me the time and opportunity to complete this task.

Lastly, I thank all my family and friends who have become a part of this book and the many who have provided inspiration and support over the years. And I thank you, dear reader, for sharing a dream and a prayer that God, by His Spirit, might keep us moving on with Him into all that the future holds for the people of God.

And, most importantly, I extend my gratitude to the Father, Son, and Holy Spirit, for He has only made a beginning with each one of us. By His grace, there will be still many chapters left to write.

Contents

Foreword

The Holy Spirit has often been associated with bizarre religious meetings, financial irresponsibility, and extravagant speech. For too long, it has seemed as if the Christians most concerned with the Holy Spirit were the Christians everyone wanted to avoid! And I can understand this—especially when the talk about power, prophecy, and visions is sometimes not grounded in godly, biblical understanding of the Christian life. There are times, no doubt, the Holy Spirit gets blamed for every pizza-induced dream.

This culture of extremes has made it hard to understand the true role of the Holy Spirit. According to the Bible, the Holy Spirit is not just something that "shows up" to give prophecies, impart healing, or fix problems. The Holy Spirit is the very being of the triune God who inhabits every believer in the world, the force of God that draws unbelievers unto Himself, the instigator of God's work everywhere, and the completer of that work in and through us every day. The Holy Spirit is no less than God Himself on earth.

This book sends a loud and clear message: The Holy Spirit is not just for Charismatics anymore! Dr. Clive Calver assures us that the Holy Spirit is by definition very much a part of the life of every believer. He gives us a clear picture of who the Spirit is, how He works, and how we can make sure that we are constantly submitting our lives to Him.

In fact, this book makes it impossible for us to neglect the Holy Spirit. Dr. Calver so thoroughly addresses the many roles the Holy Spirit plays in the Bible—from providing prophetic insight and comfort all the way to raising Jesus from the dead—that we realize there really is no Christian life apart from the Spirit of God. He proves that *to be a Christian is to flow in the Holy Spirit!*

I'm so glad that these insights are coming from Dr. Calver, because he is one of the most valuable Christian ministers working in the world today. He preaches the gospel with his life. As the president of World Relief, the relief and development arm of the National Association of Evangelicals, Dr. Calver invests his time and energy in alleviating human suffering around the world. World Relief serves in the neediest regions of the world and has been at the forefront of such issues as the AIDS epidemic in Africa and the agricultural crisis in Latin America. World Relief is a local church-based movement, which means that they don't just dump resources on problems—they address long-term problems from within. In other words, they follow the call of the Holy Spirit, go to where the Spirit is most needed, then seek to create opportunities for the Spirit to work. They save lives from the outside in. Watching World Relief work is truly a remarkable experience, and Dr. Clive Calver is truly a remarkable man.

When you meet him and spend time in his presence—either in person or through the pages of this book—you will see that his message makes absolute sense. It all fits together—who he is, what he says, and what he does. His life is organized around one basic principle: the gospel is for real. He lives it, breathes it, *is* it. Everything Dr. Calver does is an attempt to reflect how God's plan of redemption is working its way through the world.

So I trust what Dr. Calver says about the Holy Spirit. I trust him when he says that the Spirit is available for everyone in the world, that the Spirit is at work in the far reaches of the planet, and that He is transforming all kinds of lives, from the poorest child in Rwanda to the most privileged housewife in America. I trust him when he says that the purpose of the Holy Spirit is to encourage all people everywhere to become more like Jesus every day. I trust what he says, and I hope you will, too.

—TED HAGGARD, SENIOR PASTOR, NEW LIFE CHURCH
COLORADO SPRINGS, COLORADO
PRESIDENT, NATIONAL ASSOCIATION OF EVANGELICALS

1

THE MISSING PERSON
OF THE TRINITY

Rhoda sits alone each day in the dust and dirt of the streets of Lilongwe, the capital city of the southern African country of Malawi. She is blind, and because no employer will adapt a job to suit her skills, she has been forced to resort to the daily practice of begging in order to survive. Each day she is occupied with just one task: somehow eking out a frugal existence for herself and her mentally defective husband. Because it is impossible for him to work, their very survival depends on what is placed in Rhoda's tin cup each day.

Rhoda is a Christian. She is a daughter in that worldwide family that will inhabit eternity with all those who, like her, love Jesus. As she leaves the unfurnished hovel she calls "home," she senses rather than sees the people passing her by. A small baby clings to her as she makes her way to her usual place on the street corner. But the tiny squalling bundle of fragile humanity is not her daughter but her granddaughter. Rhoda's own daughter died of AIDS when the infant was only a few days old. Now the blind grandmother is the only one left to care for the baby, a child almost certainly infected with the HIV virus herself.

On the morning that my wife, Ruth, encountered Rhoda, the poor, blind beggar woman had just discovered that her water jar had been stolen from her side. It had been her only earthly possession.

In her usual straightforward style, Ruth asked a profound and

1

significant question: "Do you have any message you'd like me to take back from Africa to your brothers and sisters in the West?"

"Yes, there is something I would like you to tell them," came the immediate reply. "I want you to pass along the message that Rhoda is doing well and that all is fine for me here. Please say to my brothers and sisters that I have everything I could need, because I have Jesus."

You and I may marvel at the simple faith of this saint of God. We may wonder how it is that someone who possesses so few material possessions could feel so spiritually blessed. How could it be that someone who has been deprived of so much can cling so tenaciously to the conviction that she is truly loved by God and that the Lord's presence is with her?

The answer is simple and straightforward: her faith is supernatural in origin. Such tenacious belief—despite such terrible circumstances—can only be accounted for by the work of the Holy Spirit. It would certainly take a provision of divine strength and enabling for Rhoda to exhibit such supreme faith and confidence in the presence and power of Jesus working in her life.

GOD IS THE ONLY EXPLANATION

The consistent demonstration of such dramatic qualities can originate only in the Holy Spirit Himself. He has been called "the author of every positive revolution in the history of the church," "Satan's unsolved problem," and "God's secret weapon, bringing explosive life to His people."

All of these descriptions may be accurate, but the sad truth is that during long periods of Christian history, the Holy Spirit has more often been regarded as a silent partner, the forgotten member of the Trinity. Too often He has received little or no acknowledgment of His power and role in the lives of believers. At times, He even appears to have been almost excluded from the Godhead altogether, at least subconsciously, if nothing else.

This is a strange and unsatisfactory verdict to be made against the Person of the Trinity who communicates the love and presence of God. This is no mere external communication, for the Holy Spirit actually takes up residence within the lives of those who have surrendered to the forgiveness and saving love of Jesus Christ. In the final analysis, the Holy Spirit is no less than the very Presence of the living God making His home in the life of the believer.

The problem is that Christians generally find it easier to understand and relate to God the Father and God the Son, but they find it much harder to grasp the concept of God the Holy Spirit. While it is relatively easy to wrap our minds around a Father who creates or the Son who walked in history, the notion of an indefinable entity who comes from God to live within His people is another matter entirely. But the Holy Spirit is actually the Person of the Godhead who takes up residence within our lives, and because He cannot be separated from the Father and the Son, He brings them along!

The story is told of a pastor's visit to a Sunday school class. The children had prepared for his visit, and each had been allocated a portion of the catechism to recite. One after the other, they proceeded until a silence interrupted the flow where the words "I believe in the Holy Spirit" should have been spoken. Eventually one child offered the explanation, "Sorry, Pastor, the boy who believes in the Holy Spirit isn't here this morning!"

Sometimes we are content to go about our lives in a similar way. Tragically, our struggle to understand the nature and character of the Holy Spirit has often resulted in our unconsciously but effectively deleting Him from the Trinity. But the Holy Spirit is the One who draws us near to God; He is the Person who lives in us and is intimately connected with our lives.

The wonder of the Christian gospel is that there is one God, the Creator and Ruler of heaven and earth—and He has no intention of keeping His distance! The living God is prepared to come and live in our hearts and lives through His Holy Spirit, who comes to actually "indwell" us! It is this amazing reality that made the apostle Paul gasp in astonishment at the wonder of "the glorious riches of this mystery, which is Christ in you, the hope of glory" (Col. 1:27).

A god who was content just to remain "out there" could not be the Lord of glory. He would be little more than some impersonal cosmic force dictating instructions to our minor planet.

Most people could never be content with a God who only makes "guest appearances" on the planet He once created. Who would want a deity who only interfered in our world from time to time and then quickly retreated, withdrawing to a safe distance from which He could observe current developments in peace and quiet?

Who could be satisfied with a God who only revealed Himself through a manuscript He had written? We want to do more than read letters about Him or read narratives about what He once said and did—the yearning of the human heart is to know Him for ourselves, not yesterday, but in the here and now.

Instead, salvation came in the person and personality of Jesus! And even after His ascension into heaven, Jesus still left the power and the presence of His Holy Spirit to fill the lives of His disciples while they remained on the earth.

Most Christians would never accept the idea of a God who is only "out there somewhere," some impersonal cosmic force dictating instructions to our minor planet, or even a God who was content merely to reveal Himself through the pages of a book. Most Christians would also reject the image of a deity who only interferes from time to time, making an occasional brief excursion into time and space, only to retreat quickly to a safe distance from where He can observe current developments by remote control. No Christian can conceive of God as one who demands belief and faith while hiding in a corner of the universe, determined to remain unknown and unknowable. Our God is one whose greatest desire is for a relationship with human beings.

That is why God walked and talked with Adam in the Garden of Eden (Gen. 3:8–9).

That is why God took Israel to be His people in a covenant relationship (Deut. 4:32–35).

That is why God spoke to His people through His servants the prophets, and why He continued to send prophets even though they were rejected one after another (Ezek. 2:1–7).

The Missing Person of the Trinity

That is why God sent John the Baptist to prepare His people for the imminent birth of His only begotten Son, Jesus Christ (John 1:7). That is why Jesus came, fully God and fully man, born to be laid in a cattle trough in a dirty Bethlehem stable (Luke 2:7). That is why Jesus revealed His Father's love, fulfilling His mission by dying on a real cross at the hands of real men on a Jerusalem rubbish dump, breaking the power of sin and death (Luke 23:33).

There is something so wonderful about the way that God wants to become intimately involved with people. Folk religions are full of stories about arbitrary, capricious, transcendent beings, "gods" who were briefly involved in the real world, only to withdraw quickly in disgust. The truth is, Jesus was totally different. He portrayed the love of His Father in a radical and unusual light. He identified with His people. He ate, drank, spoke, experienced hunger and thirst, ran out of money, became tired, and eventually died at the hands of occupying forces.

As Scripture points out:

> Since the children have flesh and blood, he [Jesus] too shared in their humanity so that by his death he might destroy him who holds the power over death—that is, the devil—and free those who all their lives were held in slavery.
> —HEBREWS 2:14–15

This one true living God, the Creator of heaven and earth, the Creator of each universe and galaxy, has truly come to us. And even greater still, He continues to come to us today. God Himself actually wants to dwell in us, to live His life within ours. The apostle Paul makes it clear that at the moment we turn from living for ourselves and surrender the control of our lives to God, a miracle occurs. He declares, "The Spirit of God lives in you" (Rom. 8:9). Paul explains how this happens when he adds, "God's Spirit joins himself to our spirits" (Rom. 8:16, GNT).

This fact clearly distinguishes Christianity from all other religions. Christianity offers what no other faith dare claim: not just information about God, man, and His world; not merely a set of standards to follow and a list of instructions to obey; but rather, an

5

introduction to God Himself! Instead of just telling us what to do, God supplies us with His Holy Spirit so that we may have the necessary spiritual power to live up to His standards. When we receive the forgiveness that Jesus died on a cross to make possible, God cleanses us from our sins and both qualifies and enables us to live as His sons and daughters.

God gives us His Spirit so that we might be supernaturally equipped to live as God Himself intended that we should. And this provides the only feasible explanation for how Rhoda can face her adverse circumstances and still live, against all odds, a truly triumphant life in Jesus!

God's offer to live in us is one to which many people, like Rhoda, have responded. Far from being distant, God desires to live with us in the most intimate relationship possible. Many of us know this to be the truth because that is exactly what has happened in our own lives.

So, why do so many misunderstandings still surround the workings of the Holy Spirit? Unanswered questions, coupled with fear and doubt, can create problems, especially for new believers. But the Holy Spirit's activity within each believer is a vital prerequisite to engaging in fruitful service to God Himself. It would be idiotic to suggest that we could ever be content with serving God in our own strength. The plain and simple fact is that when it comes to living for God, we cannot do it alone.

2

WITHOUT THE SPIRIT

A close friend of mine was speaking to a group of Christian leaders at a large conference. He began to challenge them about the role of the Holy Spirit within their church communities. He concluded, as many others have, that if the Spirit were to be taken from us, 95 percent of our church activities would go on exactly as before! At the end of the session, a question was asked. One of the leaders wanted to know how to structure the local church so that the other 5 percent would be covered as well!

The problem is that far too many of us have become suspicious of the Spirit. It is one of the great tragedies of the American church that we have devised so many ways and means of managing without the Holy Spirit. We have replaced Him in so many areas with human expertise and other resources. Instead of filling up at the premium gasoline pump, we have concentrated on inventing our own substandard bootleg fuel! And in our struggle to find ways of coping alone, we have totally ignored God's magnificent provision for us.

In his excellent book *Why Revival Tarries*, Leonard Ravenhill succinctly summarized the tragic way in which many of us are content to live: "Warned of false fire by fireless men, we so often settle for no fire at all."[1]

"DO NOT ENTER"

When driving down the road, at times we will encounter a sign that says, "Do Not Enter." The message is quite plain: this is an area in which we should not drive. In the same way, there are certain things we should never do with the Christian faith, places we should not "enter."

- The Christian life should never be reduced to the level of rote obedience, to a list of legal instructions.

- Christianity should not be shrunk down to a set of routines or rituals that we follow like slaves.

- Christianity is not a New Age process of finding the inner self or unlocking the secret to the destiny of humankind.

- Christianity is not merely a process of coming to know ourselves better.

These ideas fall within the territories of other faiths. The claims of Christianity have always been much higher than such limited notions. For evangelical Christians, the message of the Christian faith is plain and direct, and it is revealed in the Bible: God came to earth as a man, demonstrated what life could be, and died on a cross to forgive and recover a people for Himself.

Despite constant rejections throughout history, the living God has continued to stretch out His hands of love toward His people throughout the length and breadth of His world. As the Creator, He loved the world enough to allow His Son, Jesus, to die for us all. Having conquered the grave, Jesus now reigns at His Father's right hand in the glory of heaven, and we eagerly await God's final act in history—the taking of His own people to be with Him forever.

Unfortunately, humankind has never fully cooperated with God's plan. People consistently reject God's will and purposes. God desires that all would commit their lives to Jesus, receive His forgiveness, and spend eternity with Him.

The Holy Spirit has been sent from within the Godhead as a

divine gift to all who respond to the love of Jesus and confess Him as their Lord and King. He has been given to help us grow in our Christian lives and bear the witness of Jesus to the world. The Holy Spirit brings the life and power of Jesus into our lives so that we too might become more like Jesus. Put simply, the Spirit-filled life of Jesus becomes ours, and He is the One who is at work within us, preparing us for an eternal relationship with Him.

This is God's gift of love, given to us because He knows that we cannot make it in our Christian lives without Him. Instead of giving us some vague "force" to which we cannot relate, He equips us with His very own Spirit. But because the Holy Spirit is at one with God the Father and God the Son, we need a greater understanding of the relationship between the members of the Trinity. Because our minds are only human, we will never comprehend the divine fully, but we should do what we can.

Augustine, one of the fathers of the early church, wrote the earliest systematic treatment of the subject as part of his fifteen-volume work *On the Trinity*. Since then, most Christian scholars have agreed on these fundamental truths:

- No person of the Trinity is superior or inferior to any other.

- Christianity does not acknowledge three gods but one God, for the Persons of the Trinity are one in nature and glory, and they work harmoniously for our salvation.

If all this sounds rather puzzling, don't be alarmed! There are many things that we will never grasp completely. After all, if we knew all there was to know about God, He would hardly be worth knowing! Our finite minds were never intended to understand the infinite God. If we could, our God would be reduced to human dimensions, and He would be far too small.

Although God the Father took the initiative in Creation, He did not act alone, for the Son and Spirit were involved as well. Neither has the Son or Spirit acted alone since that time. They are all three intimately bonded together in an eternal union. So today, when the Holy Spirit comes into our lives, He does not enter alone. He always brings the Father and the Son with Him.

When we pray, it is generally to the Father, through the Son, but in the Holy Spirit. To emphasize this threefold nature of God, Paul delivered this simple blessing over the Corinthian church: "May the grace of the Lord Jesus Christ, and the love of God, and the fellowship of the Holy Spirit be with you all" (2 Cor. 13:14).

MISSING OUT ON THE REAL THING

We have already said that we could not be expected to serve God properly if we were simply confined to our own limited human resources. So if we were without the Spirit, just where would we be?

1. Without the Holy Spirit, there would be no *witness*. Without the Spirit, we would be left with only our own resources for serving Jesus and sharing His love with others. The disciples were told not to attempt *anything* until they had received power from the Holy Spirit. "But you will receive power when the Holy Spirit comes on you; and you will be my witnesses in Jerusalem, and in all Judea and Samaria, and to the ends of the earth" (Acts 1:8).

2. Without the Holy Spirit, there would be no *understanding*. Without the Spirit, we could not learn all that God longs to teach us. The Holy Spirit wants to share with us all that we need to know. He is uniquely qualified to do this because "only God's Spirit knows all about God" (1 Cor. 2:11, GNT).

3. Without the Holy Spirit, there would be no *worship*. Without the Spirit, our worship would be little more than a mere routine expression to God. As Jesus taught the Samaritan woman at the well, "God is Spirit, and only by the power of his Spirit can people worship him as he really is" (John 4:24, GNT).

4. Without the Holy Spirit, there would be no *gifts*. Without the Spirit, we could not receive from the Lord the spiritual gifts He wants to give to properly equip us for His service. "The man without the Spirit does not accept the things that come from the Spirit of God" (1 Cor. 2:14).

5. Without the Holy Spirit, there would be no *power*. If we were challenged by God to live His life yet not given the power to do so, all our Christian lives would amount to no more than the sum total of our maximum human efforts. The Holy Spirit introduces a totally different dimension, a source of power for living, that emanates from God Himself and changes us into radically different people. "For God did not give us a spirit of timidity, but a spirit of power, of love and of self-discipline" (2 Tim. 1:7).

6. Without the Holy Spirit, there would be no *guidance*. If we did not have the Holy Spirit, we would be devoid of a real revelation of all that God has prepared for us, and we would remain trapped in the confines of our own ambitions. We must rely on the Holy Spirit to show us what to do. When, for example, Paul and his companions wanted to go into Bithynia, "the Spirit of Jesus would not allow them to" (Acts 16:7).

7. Without the Holy Spirit, there would be no *security*. The Holy Spirit is God's "guarantee" to us that God will take care of us now and in the future. "This is how we know that he lives in us: We know it by the Spirit he gave us" (1 John 3:24). Time and again, the Holy Spirit is referred to as the "Spirit of truth" who fulfills God's promises to His people.

8. Without the Holy Spirit, there would be no *evidence*. Without the Spirit, we would have no supernatural

11

demonstration of God's reality and power. These miraculous events were never just the special province of the apostles. We read, for example, that "Stephen, a man full of faith and the Holy Spirit...a man full of God's grace and power, did great wonders and miraculous signs among the people" (Acts 6:5, 8).

9. Without the Holy Spirit, there would be no *life*. The Spirit brings a quality of life that is its own testimony to the world in which God has placed us. "The mind controlled by the Spirit is life and peace" (Rom. 8:6).

10. Without the Holy Spirit, there would be no *future*. We have something to look forward to because we know that God "has set his seal of ownership on us, and put his Spirit in our hearts as a deposit, guaranteeing what is to come" (2 Cor. 1:22).

11. Without the Holy Spirit, there would be no *uniqueness*. There are so many other religions and faiths that claim to bring information about God and man, about the past and the future. But for Christians, the Holy Spirit makes all the difference. Instead of just *talking about* a God who is out there somewhere, we *know* Him, and He lives within us! What is more, He is the Holy Spirit. The Greek word translated *holy* implies a meaning of "being different."[2] The Holy Spirit alone can take ordinary lives and work a transformation within them.

12. Without the Holy Spirit, there would be no *obedience*. True obedience from the heart is something that only God can bring. As we live in obedience to His direction, we don't discover an easy route, but we do find a God who never leaves us. "Now, in obedience to the Holy Spirit I am going to Jerusalem.... The Holy Spirit has warned me that prison and troubles wait for me. But I reckon my own life to be worth

nothing to me; I only want to complete my mission and finish the work that the Lord Jesus gave me to do" (Acts 20:22–24, GNT).

13. Without the Holy Spirit, there would be no *resurrection*. Without the Holy Spirit, Jesus would still be dead! Christianity would not even exist. The Holy Spirit is not an "optional extra" but a crucial member of an undivided Trinity. Without the Spirit, not only would Jesus still be dead, but also we would have no hope of a future glorified body. As Paul stated, "If the Spirit of him who raised Jesus from death is living in you, he who raised Christ from the dead will also give life to your mortal bodies through his Spirit, who lives in you" (Rom. 8:11).

WHERE WOULD WE BE?

Where would we be without the Holy Spirit? Certainly nowhere good! It is tragic that for so long many Christians have relegated the Holy Spirit to the fringes of their lives when there is so much that He has done for us and still wants to do within us. It is little wonder that Satan has worked so hard to create division and confusion about the role of the Spirit. Somehow he does not mind us having head knowledge about Jesus as long as he can prevent us from enjoying the life of Jesus revealed by the Holy Spirit within us. Satan would love for us to neglect the Spirit!

Paul, James, Peter, and John all wrote about the Holy Spirit in their letters. They wrote of the fruit of the Spirit, the gifts of the Spirit, and the Spirit's work of guarding, resurrecting, witnessing, outpouring love, renewing, interceding, demonstrating, imparting gifts, giving life, transforming, sealing, promising, sanctifying, prophesying, and inspiring Scripture. With all these wonderful benefits, why would we ever want to leave Him out of our church life and teaching—indeed, in many cases, from every area of our lives?

Some years ago a wife joined her husband on a business trip to a big city. He was gone most of the day, and she was lonely. She turned to daydreaming and fantasizing to fill the long hours. All day long, while he conducted delicate financial negotiations, she was filled with a growing sense of frustration. Later that night, she surrendered to the temptation of thinking about other men. Thoughts of new partners and how they would treat her better, plus the magic of discovering forbidden love, filled her mind. In the middle of the night, she crawled out of bed and left her husband behind, disappearing into the night to fulfill her fantasies.

Several hours later she returned, having satisfied herself in a secret liaison. She slipped back into bed. A few minutes later, the husband awoke to find his wife crying uncontrollably by his side.

"What's the matter?" he asked.

She could give no reply. How could she say anything? How could she explain the most tragic moment of all—the moment when you hope to experience the "ultimate" sensation and it lets you down.

Sadly there are some who view Christianity in this way. They may have made a response to the love of Jesus, but when they woke up the next morning, they discovered that little had changed. Their expectations of a life filled only with love and joy were dashed; the unfulfilled promises now seemed to possess a hollow ring. The emotion of the moment, the experience, had seemed so undeniably real, but what, if anything, did it really mean?

The young wife had been conned, taken in by the lie that fools so many. What is that lie? The idea that ultimate truth lies in the next experience...do something forbidden, and your life will be filled with excitement...go ahead; live by your feelings. Reality never lives up to these expectations, and all such lies eventually bring failure, disappointment, and shame.

Tragically, the lives of many Christians can be just like that. Most of us would hate to admit it, but Christianity may have proved to be a little disappointing to many of us. The initial moment of commitment may have seemed so real. Our initial surrender to Jesus was utterly genuine, but somehow we missed the radical transformation that should have followed on the heels of our decision. And we struggle to live up to our promises.

We have found that knowing about God has not proved adequate to enable us to live up to His standards. Our Christian lives may resemble a two-thousand-piece jigsaw puzzle that we started to put together, only to discover that half the pieces are missing!

That is exactly what life would be like without the Holy Spirit. But the great and gloriously liberating truth is this: God did not design life to be lived this way! Instead, He has provided His Holy Spirit, who introduces us to life in a whole new dimension.

WHO IS THIS HOLY SPIRIT?

As a relatively young Christian, I began to question, "Why do I have so many failures and inadequacies in my Christian experience?" I became deeply troubled at the poverty of my own spiritual walk with God. So much of what I knew was mere information *about* God, without having much of a direct relationship *with* Him. My heart longed to have an experience like Thomas Carlyle, who spoke of what it meant to know God "other than by hearsay."[1]

I began to wonder why so many other Christians seemed to know more of the indwelling love of Jesus than I did. Why did their lives display the fruits of His grace and demonstrate His power at work within them in ways that seemed sorely lacking in my own life?

I was soon to discover that I was not alone in my frustration.

SEARCHING FOR REALITY

I was amazed when I discovered that there were many others who felt just as I did! One such person was named Bill. Bill would have called himself "average"; in many ways he was just like the rest of us. But when he committed his life to Jesus Christ, he began to feel that he was "special" in the eyes of God. He was struck by the realization that God actually "liked" him!

Bill became determined to serve the Lord. He tried very hard to do everything in just the right way, and gradually the sense of frustration and failure crept in. Friends told him it was normal, but Bill didn't think that was right. But instead of success, his personal failures continued to multiply. The early joy of his salvation faded, and a bitter, pervasive sense of disappointment took its place. Somehow, for Bill, Christianity hadn't turned out at all to be what he had hoped for.

It is so easy for us to be horrified at such a story. But if God longs to live in our lives, why do so many of us seem to end up so far away from Him?

When I was a relatively new Christian, it was hard for me to fathom how some Christians could be so different from others. Some overflowed with love and compassion for their neighbors, while others cloistered themselves away from the world, apparently fearful of contamination. Some seemed to exude a deep sense of inner joy, but others looked as if they had just received a death sentence rather than the blessing of eternal life. Some were on fire with expectancy that God would do great things in their lives; others seemed content to make survival their primary objective.

But the biggest struggle that I faced as a young Christian was determining what I believed about the Person and work of the Holy Spirit. I began to encounter Christians for whom He was a vibrant reality in their lives, a Person to know and to love, not some vague, generic "force."

WHO IS THIS HOLY SPIRIT?

If we want to discover who the Holy Spirit really is, then individual human experience is not the right place to start. When God intended to reveal His nature, will, and identity to humankind, He determined to do so supremely in His Son. When He wanted to record His activities with the inhabitants of this planet, He chose to do so in a divinely inspired Book. If we want to know what the Spirit of God is like and how He operates within the lives of the people of God, then it is to the pages of the Bible that we must first turn.

It has been pointed out—correctly, in fact—that many Christians have produced an artificial Trinity of the Father, Son, and Holy Scripture. But while the Bible is the Word of God, without error in all that it affirms, and is truly God-breathed, Scripture itself affirms that it is the Holy Spirit who is the third member of the Trinity. Throughout the pages of the Bible, it is assumed that the Holy Spirit is no more and no less than God Himself. He is called "the Spirit of the Lord" (1 Kings 18:12) and "the Spirit of Jesus" (Acts 16:7). In Luke 11:13, Jesus refers to Him as the gift of the Father. Paul clearly announced that "the Lord is the Spirit" (2 Cor. 3:17). When Peter rebuked Ananias for his attempted deception, he boldly announced the simple fact, "You have lied to the Holy Spirit.... You have not lied to men but to God" (Acts 5:3–4). On the occasion that Jesus spoke about the "unforgivable sin," He described it as blaspheming, or speaking against or rejecting, not the Father or even Jesus Himself, but the Holy Spirit (Matt. 12:31–32). It is important to note that we can "mock" or "curse" our fellow human beings, but "blasphemy" is a sin that can only be committed against God Himself.

It is because the Holy Spirit is God that Scripture describes Him as possessing all the essential characteristics that are the sole privilege of God Himself. He is:

Holy

God cannot deny His own character; therefore, in the same way that God is completely pure and totally unblemished, so must be His Holy Spirit (1 Cor. 6:19).

Eternal

If God were limited by time and space, He could not, by definition, be God. The Creator can neither be limited by His creation, nor can He die or face extinction. To be God, He must always have been God and must inhabit eternity. When Scripture says that the Holy Spirit is eternal (always was and always will be), then it is affirming that He is God (Heb. 9:14).

18

Omnipotent

The Holy Spirit is all-powerful, an attribute that is the sole province of God Himself (Luke 1:35–37).

Omnipresent

The Holy Spirit exists everywhere simultaneously. There is no place in heaven, earth, or anywhere else in the universe that is not inhabited by the Holy Spirit (Ps. 139:7).

Omniscient

The Holy Spirit knows everything that there is to know (1 Cor. 2:10–11).

These supreme qualities of the Holy Spirit are neatly summarized in Isaiah's prophecy of the anticipated Messiah:

> The Spirit of the LORD will rest upon him—the Spirit of wisdom and of understanding, the Spirit of counsel and of power, the Spirit of knowledge and of the fear of the LORD.
>
> —ISAIAH 11:2

God is personal. He neither rules nor communicates by remote control, and He possesses personality. So it is with the Holy Spirit. It would be wrong to view Him as an indefinably nebulous force. "He" is not an "it"! God the Father refers to Him as "my Spirit" (Gen. 6:3; Isa. 59:21).

The Holy Spirit is the "breath" or "wind" of God (Isa. 40:7). In the New Testament, the Greek word used to describe this is *pneuma*, which literally has those two meanings. In this sense, it might be easy to picture the Holy Spirit as something broad and vague. Yet this phrase in Scripture often brings into grammatical play a definite article; instead of "a breath" or "a wind," He is called "*the* Spirit" or "*the* Holy Spirit."

His personhood is also affirmed in that He can be grieved, He comes upon individuals at particular times, He is the means by which God fills His people, and He can even be withdrawn from them under exceptional circumstances (Eph. 4:30; Judg. 14:6; 2 Kings 2:9; Exod. 35:31; Mic. 3:8; Ps. 51:11).

The Holy Spirit is no mere arm or leg of God. He is a Person in His own right, yet He exists as part of the Godhead. He is not remote, but He actually dwells in God's people and is therefore personal to each one of us. To reinforce this point, the apostle John referred to the Holy Spirit by using a masculine pronoun (*ekeinos*, "He") with a neutral noun (*pneuma*, "Spirit"). This may seem like bad grammar to us, but it is superb theology! He does this to show that the Holy Spirit is a "He," not an "it." (See John 14:26; 15:26; 16:8–14.)

THE PERSONALITY OF THE HOLY SPIRIT

Let us take this one step farther. The vivid imagination of George Lucas, the creator of *Star Wars*, conceived of a vast "force" that could empower us and be used for either good or evil. This force was "personal" in that it was available for human personality, but it lacked "personhood" in itself. That is precisely how the Holy Spirit differs—He is not here for us to use, but we are here for Him to use to bring glory to Jesus through our lives.

Not only is the Holy Spirit personal, but also He possesses a unique personality. The three basic characteristics of personality are our innate capacity for feeling, knowing, and doing—and you may be surprised to learn that the Holy Spirit is actively engaged in all three! Scripture affirms that:

- He feels (Eph. 4:30).
- He knows (John 14:26).
- He does things (John 16:8–11).

While it is important to note that the Holy Spirit is like us in that He has a personality, it is also important to recognize that, unlike us, He is, in fact, holy. The Greek word used to describe this is *hagios*, and its root meaning is "different."[2] In this sense, He can never be as we are, and it demonstrates the grace and mercy of God that He allows His Holy Spirit to dwell in unclean human beings. The very title *Holy Spirit* indicates that this Spirit is totally different from us because He is, in fact, divine.

However, while God is one, He exists as the Trinity (Matt. 28:19; John 14:26; 15:26; 2 Cor. 13:14; 1 Pet. 1:2). Jesus revealed this supreme mystery of the Christian faith when He declared the name in which His followers should be baptized. The word used by Jesus for *name* is singular, indicating that there is only one God, but this "name" is tri-personal, because each one of us is baptized in "the name of the Father and of the Son and of the Holy Spirit" (Matt. 28:19).

In the Book of Revelation, the apostle John begins his letter to the seven churches in an unusual way, with a greeting that places God the Father first, God the Spirit second, and God the Son third (Rev. 1:4–5). While this order might seem unusual to us, the phraseology gives the standard implication that these three are inextricably intertwined and always coequal.

GOD IN ACTION

Because most Christians do find it more difficult to visualize and personalize the Holy Spirit, they often overlook the amount of work in which the Holy Spirit is engaged. He is very busy indeed! The Holy Spirit definitely understands the concept of "multi-tasking," for while He is the corporate Holy Spirit of the universal church, He is also the One who dwells in the life of every individual believer (1 Cor. 12:13; Rom. 8:9–11).

The Holy Spirit is always busy. He works within us to bring the conviction of sin, the recognition of the need for righteousness, and an awareness of impending judgment long before we come to the point of conversion and surrendering our life to Jesus Christ (John 16:8). We may not realize it, we may never even be aware of it, but quietly and invisibly, the Holy Spirit is already at work in our lives, preparing us to be confronted with the reality of Jesus Christ.

In the New Testament accounts of the conversions of Zacchaeus, Cornelius, and that unnamed Ethiopian eunuch to whom Philip witnessed of Jesus Christ, the Holy Spirit was actively at work preparing the ground for their moments of truth! In the case of the Ethiopian eunuch, He even called Philip away from a revival and into the desert to explain the Scriptures to the eunuch at just the right time.

When we come to Christ, the Holy Spirit makes His home in our lives. He is the giver of new life, and He becomes the seal and evidence of our salvation, as we see in John 3:5; 2 Corinthians 1:22; Titus 3:5; and especially Romans 8:9–11. And it is the Holy Spirit who then takes on the raw material of the new convert's heart and begins the often lengthy process of transforming it into the image of the Lord Jesus.

This whole idea of an indwelling Holy Spirit who inhabits the life of every believer introduced to the world a concept unknown in other major religions. For the first time, God was not just "out there somewhere," but He could be intimately known, loved, and served. Christianity is offering not a *religion* about God, but a *relationship* with Him.

4

THE LIVING GOD IS AT WORK!

Knowing what you want is one thing, but acquiring it for yourself can be another matter entirely. I always had difficulty reconciling myself to the fact that I found it easier to identify with those who spoke in impersonal terms about the Holy Spirit than with those who seemed to see His vital presence at work within their daily lives. So many people seemed to be making such extravagant claims about the activity of the Holy Spirit in their lives that I began to wonder if I were losing out somewhere, or if others were simply deluding themselves.

Or perhaps I was lacking in some area of living in the power and authority of the Holy Spirit. I began to look for the answers to my questions, but when I sought an explanation, my suspicions became aroused. I had attended seminary, and I knew a great deal *about* the Holy Spirit. But all my studies seemed to do was cause confusion. There was no one perspective or single viewpoint. One view challenged another until all that was left was division, disagreement, and dispute.

I knew that the subject was vitally important; some people had even claimed that the way Christians lived could be directly attributed to the quality of their relationship with the Holy Spirit. This seemed to be too simple an explanation, but I knew there had to be more to Christianity than mere belief. I had to find out what it meant for God to live within me.

BE CAREFUL—GOD IS AT WORK!

That questioning phase in my life took place several years ago. Since then I have often had the privilege of watching the Holy Spirit's work in practice. This has usually been at its most obvious in the lives of the poorest of the poor and of those who live and work among them.

The living God is at work—often where we would least expect to find Him.

Silviane lives in Haiti. She was only sixteen years old when she was raped. The perpetrator was the man for whom she worked as a domestic servant. These "domestic servants" were known as *restereki*, a polite way of referring to people who were virtual slaves, forced to do whatever their master required. She left the house immediately after this atrocity, but two or three months later, she discovered, to her horror, that she was pregnant as a result of the rape. After the birth, she suddenly had a child to look after, and the only way she knew to survive was through prostitution. She would sell her body for ten Haitian gourdes, around two dollars, but the inevitable result was that she bore more children from unknown fathers. In order to feed her family, she soon found it necessary to work the streets all day long.

After six years of this lifestyle, Silviane was occupying a little shack in a vast slum. This slum was called "City Soleil," and it was probably the most infamous of the ironically named slums that are "home" to several thousand of Haiti's poorest people. The slum was adjacent to the headquarters of the Lemuel Project, an indigenous evangelical organization that offered care and support for those living in squalid conditions. Its director, a warm and approachable Haitian named Manis, had a simple rule for the staff members who were involved with the project. He insisted that there was to be no direct verbal "evangelism" until a person initiated such a discussion. His conviction was that truly Christian lives would provoke questions based on the example they provided.

The only exception to this rule Manis felt obligated to make was in witnessing to those suffering from AIDS or some other chronic disease; because they might not have much time left, they are told of Jesus immediately.

Gigi, an American nurse who had lived in Haiti for thirty-seven years, met and befriended Silviane. After several months, Silviane eventually asked the bitter and honest question, "What are you trying to get from me?" Gigi's opportunity had come! She responded that rather than trying to exploit Silviane, Gigi was trying to give her something. And she led Silviane to commit her life to Jesus.

Today, Silviane's home is still the same tiny, primitive hut in the shantytown of Port-au-Prince, Haiti. The entire dwelling consists of a single room that she shares with her five children. Because Silviane is given to hospitality and is reluctant to see anyone left on the street, at times as many as eight people will be housed in that one room "constructed" from discarded pieces of used plywood and tin. One night at her weekly small-group fellowship meeting, Silviane wanted everyone to share her joy and thank the Lord with her. The reason for her excitement was that she had discovered a brand-new sheet of tin—without holes—and she at last had a small corner of her room where she could sit and not get wet when it rained.

Many of us would ask what could possibly have brought such joy and peace to the lives of Manis, Silviane, and Gigi.

How could Silviane be so happy at receiving so little?

How could Gigi experience such contentment in her mission field—one of the worst slums on earth?

How could the message of Jesus actually be expressed without words?

How could Christians find the joy of the Lord when living in such appalling conditions?

The answer can only lie in a supernatural power, the power of God Himself. To state it plainly: the Holy Spirit makes it possible. It was St. Francis of Assisi who often said, "Preach the Gospel at all times. If necessary, use words." Now this may cause many of us difficulties, but in the case of Manis, it became reality. He did not seek to excuse his faith or deny his faith, but he knew that sometimes the visible reality comes through with a powerful effectiveness that would be denied to mere words. That is always something that can only happen when it is the Holy Spirit who is doing the living through us.

In a life that is truly Christian, the Holy Spirit does all the work; we just cooperate. Instead of hopelessly trying to live up to a list of commands, the Christian realizes that God Himself provides the means to live up to His own demands: His Holy Spirit. (See Romans 8.) The Spirit is actively working on, through, and in our lives. What will ultimately emerge is a transformed character.

DANGER—LIVES ARE BEING CHANGED!

This radically changed lifestyle is demonstrated by the fruit of the Holy Spirit, which Paul listed in Galatians 5:22–23, in the life of the believer. Love, joy, peace, patience, kindness, goodness, faithfulness, gentleness, and self-control certainly indicate that a change has taken place! But these are all part and parcel of the same character transformation. Some have said that there is just one fruit—and it comes in nine different flavors! When patience begins to work its way in our life, we experience more peace, joy, goodness, and so on. Each "flavor" of fruit promotes the others.

The presence of the Holy Spirit in our lives allows us to demonstrate each aspect of His fruit in equal measure. We can see this in the different ways that the Holy Spirit works in our lives and in our world. Even a brief glance makes the enormous size and scope of His workload, which includes the following, become obvious.

- Bringing the reality of the Father to us (Rom. 8:15)
- Inspiring and revealing truth (1 Sam. 10:10; John 16:13)
- Assuring each one of us of the permanence and security of our relationship with Jesus (Rom. 8:16)
- Glorifying Jesus (John 16:14)

26

The Living God Is at Work!

- Providing leadership (Ps. 143:10; Acts 13:2; Rom. 8:14)
- Removing fear (2 Tim. 1:7)
- Helping us respond to God and His love for us (Ps. 51:10–12; Ezek. 36:25–27; Joel 2:28–29)
- Making Jesus real to us (Acts 7:55)
- Working in the creation of the world (Gen. 1:2; Job 33:4)
- Indwelling the lives of individuals (Rom. 8:9)
- Indwelling the life of the church (1 Cor. 2:12)
- Helping us anticipate the future life (2 Cor. 5:5)
- Praying through us (Eph. 6:18)
- Bringing the conviction of sin and providing the power to overcome it (John 16:8–10; Rom. 8:13)
- Transmitting creative skills to human beings (Exod. 31:1–11; 1 Kings 7:14)
- Controlling the course of nature and human history (Ps. 104:29–30; Isa. 34:16; 40:7)
- Strengthening us (Eph. 3:16)
- Providing instruction and confirming the truth of God (John 15:26; Acts 11:12; 1 Cor. 2:12)
- Engaging in spiritual warfare through us (Eph. 6:17)
- Filling our lives (Acts 4:31; Eph. 5:18)

Some of us may wonder how God can reside in each one of us at the same time. Surely He would have to divide up the Holy Spirit to make this possible, wouldn't He? But God's infinite nature makes this unnecessary. As one perceptive twentieth-century voice observed, "An infinite God can give all of himself to each of his children. He does not distribute himself that all may have a part, but to each he gives all of himself as fully as if there were no others."[1]

In other words, we do not have to "share"—in the sense of dividing—the Holy Spirit with others. We can each possess all of Him that there is to have. Everywhere we go, we can be assured of the presence of the Holy Spirit (Ps. 139:7). He becomes the controlling influence within us and acts as our guide and spiritual director. He empowers us for service, and He instructs us in all that we need to know. The Holy Spirit is the deposit and guarantee of eternal life. He acts as the promise of all that is to come, and He stays with us forever. With all these benefits, it is easier to understand why Jesus assured His disciples that it was to their advantage for Him to go away and for His Spirit to come.

And it is indeed *His* Spirit.

THE SPIRIT OF JESUS

Jesus was conceived by the Holy Spirit, born to perform the will of the Father (Luke 1:32–35). Immediately following His baptism, Jesus was anointed by the Holy Spirit as the Father spoke from heaven (Matt. 3:16–17). The ministry of the Holy Spirit reveals Jesus to men and women, and Jesus, in turn, shows His Father to them (John 14:9, 26). This same Holy Spirit was Christ's gift to all believers, enabling them to live in the way that He intended for them, fulfilling the mission that He had given to them (Acts 2:32–33).

One of the single most perplexing questions in the Bible is how 120 frightened, cowering followers of Jesus, barely clinging to their own existence, could be suddenly transformed into an army of men and women who effectively turned their world upside down with the gospel. One moment they were huddling together for survival; the next they were charging out into the world, ready to change the destiny of humankind. Armed with no weapons other than their own naked confidence in the will of God, they persuaded stalwart inhabitants of the Roman empire that a dead carpenter had risen from the dead. Not only that, but He also opened the doors of forgiveness and eternity to all who would surrender the control of their lives into His nail-pierced hands.

The Living God Is at Work!

These believers' lives predated the era of air transport, information technology, and global communication. Traveling primarily by foot, their progress was frustratingly slow. Regularly they faced the perils of bandits and disease, shipwrecks and hostile authorities, constantly risking life and limb to spread the Good News. They experienced torture, imprisonment, and death, yet no persecution could extinguish the brightness of their flame. Indeed, as the early church historian Tertullian observed near the close of the second century A.D., "The blood of the martyrs is the seed of the church."[2]

How did it happen? What mysterious event took place that would cause this frightened group of disciples to give their lives and usher in a movement that would change human history? No human analysis can begin to explain how these events could have happened in the dramatic way that they did. The story *almost* requires supernatural intervention to be believable—and that is exactly what happened.

When the Holy Spirit took up permanent residence in their lives, these early Christians were able to boldly go where no one had gone before! Gripped by the powerful message of God's transforming love, they began to win the lost world for Jesus—demonstrating the exact nature of the Holy Spirit. Because of who He is, the Holy Spirit transforms ordinary people into the very hands and feet of Jesus. As God Himself, He constantly shapes the lives of God's people and brings glory to the full majesty of the Godhead.

A "new way" was begun at Pentecost. Jesus' sacrifice opened a new chapter in the story of God's dealings with humankind, and the Holy Spirit simply took hold of the lives of a group of ordinary people in order to share that message with the world. He began to transform them from who they were into who they could become.

Who is this Holy Spirit?

He is God at work in us, progressively changing us to be more and more like Jesus. He is able to take very raw material—ordinary people like you and me—and make us into people who will transform both the history of the world and the population of heaven.

LEARNING TO LIVE

A uthor Denys Parsons relates the following story in the book *The Best of Shrdlu*:

> A baby rabbit fell into a quarry's mixing machine yesterday and came out in the middle of a concrete block. But the rabbit still had the strength to dig its way free before the block set.
>
> The tiny creature was scooped up with thirty tons of sand, then swirled and pounded through the complete mixing process.... With the thirty tons of sand, it was dropped into a weighing hopper and carried by conveyor to an overhead mixer where it was whirled around with gallons of water.
>
> From there the rabbit was swept to a machine, which hammers wet concrete into blocks, by pressure of 100 pounds per square inch. The rabbit was encased in a block eighteen inches long, nine inches high and six inches thick. Finally the blocks were ejected on to the floor to dry and the dazed rabbit clawed itself free! We cleaned him up, dried him by the electric fire, then he hopped away![1]

Many people could see their own lives reflected in this story: a poor innocent caught in the vast machine of life, only just barely managing to escape. For the Christian, such a picture completely fails to capture the truth. When we gave our lives to Jesus Christ, we placed ourselves under His control. So why, then, do accidents in life occur that clearly, to our minds, could not be in the will and purpose of God?

The answer lies in the redirection the living God longs to provide for our lives. God uses unusual and mysterious courses of action to fulfill His divine purposes for us. After all, if He were content to work within our finite "categories" of action, then He would be less than who He is. It is precisely because He is God that He operates in ways that are beyond the human mind. We cannot expect Him to be content to bless whatever agenda we lay before Him. As a loving Father who knows what is best for His children, He wants us to be obedient to Him as He acts within His own will.

A MATTER OF GUIDANCE

I remember the days when my oldest son, Kris, was six years old. Whenever I came home after having been away for a few days, I found that I could suggest just about any activity to him and he would happily agree, demonstrating an unusual degree of compliance. So we could take the dog for a walk, play a game of soccer, or go shopping together in town—pretty much any suggestion I made would receive an enthusiastic, "Great, Dad!" He was so pleased to have his daddy home that he didn't care what we did, as long as we did it together. He just wanted to be with his dad.

Later in life, especially when the teenage years arrived, things began to change. Kris began to realize that he possessed a will of his own. He would express his own desires, and if they conflicted with mine, a meaningful dialogue would immediately take place! If the disagreement continued, I faced a serious choice. I could either impose my own will, or I could leave it up to my son and trust that either he or I would learn if we made a mistake.

In some ways, the relationship between my son and me is a lot like our relationship with God. However, because I am not God, the analogy naturally breaks down. Kris's course of action may actually prove to be better than what I propose. But with a loving God who is totally committed to us, that possibility does not exist. He loves us so much, and He only desires the best for His people.

God does not push His will onto us. He is no arbitrary deity just trying to get His own way, but He longs to guide us into true fulfillment in our lives. He looks for people who will trust Him to know what is best for them, people whom He can involve in the unfolding of His purposes in their nation and His world. That is why He does not leave us blindly to pursue our own pathway, but He offers Himself as the greatest Guide that we will ever know.

Even still, God leaves it in our hands to respond in obedience to the guidance He provides. It is up to us to be sensitive to Him. We are not mere robots, waiting to be "wound up," preprogrammed to conform to His will for our lives. In Psalm 32:8–9, a clear promise of guidance is accompanied by an equally clear instruction to be sensitive to His leading:

> I will instruct you and teach you in the way you should go; I will counsel you and watch over you. Do not be like the horse or the mule, which have no understanding but must be controlled with by bit and bridle or they will not come to you.

God wants to know if we wish to listen to the direction of His Spirit, or if we are stubbornly determined to stick with the folly of our own inclinations.

A PARTING GIFT

It is often so difficult to be sure when God is speaking to us; so many times we are left wondering if what we are sensing is God or just our own imagination. How can we understand what God wants us to do?

Shortly before He died, Jesus made what some consider His "last will and testament." He bequeathed His body to Joseph of Arimathea, His clothes to the soldiers who had crucified Him, His mother to His beloved disciple, John, and His Spirit to His Father, but before that day, He left to His disciples a very special promise: "Peace I leave with you; my peace I give you" (John 14:27). He appointed no executor to ensure that the provisions of His will were fulfilled; instead, He personally visited them after His resurrection to be sure that they had received His parting gift. He even walked through a solid wall in order to greet them with the words, "Peace be with you!" (John 20:19).

The leaving present of Jesus to His followers was a peace that the world can never provide, a peace that only the Holy Spirit can give. Paul commented about this peace in his letter to the Colossians: "Let the peace of Christ rule in your hearts, since as members of one body you were called to peace" (Col. 3:15).

Jesus emphasized this same truth in another marvelous promise He made to His followers: He pledged that we would not be left as orphans in a pagan world. Instead the Holy Spirit would come and "will guide you into all truth" (John 16:13). In other words, the Holy Spirit comes to direct our lives, and the peace of God rules in our hearts to confirm that guidance.

LISTENING FOR BEGINNERS

"How can I be sure?"

If I had a dollar for every time I have been asked that question, I would be a wealthy man! God's Spirit has many ways of guiding us, some more dramatic than others, but only rarely will it be as obvious as literal writing on the wall.

Despite the variety of ways in which God leads His people, there remains one common factor. It is in the intimacy of a deep, personal relationship with Jesus that we find the Holy Spirit directing our lives. As we surrender our lives in an ever-deepening commitment to Jesus and listen for the voice of His Spirit, His purposes for us become clear.

There are several common ways God makes His will known. Let's look briefly at a few of them.

Through circumstances

While this is perhaps the most common manner in which Christians receive guidance, it is notoriously unreliable. The Holy Spirit can and does guide through circumstances, but we must be certain that it is His hand that lies behind each situation. At this point we need the peace of God to act as the signal to our hearts.

Several years ago, Ruth and I found ourselves in a real dilemma as we were seeking direction for the future. Every circumstance seemed to be pointing toward one particular direction for the two of us. Yet Ruth felt a real absence of peace, a sense of disquiet brewing within her. Because of this, we proceeded with extreme caution, believing that God would either clearly confirm this check in Ruth's spirit or dismiss it. Not many days after that, the Lord let us know that we should take the matter no further. This later proved to have been the right decision. I might struggle as a man to acknowledge that my wife was right, but I have observed over the years that women are often more sensitive and open to divine direction than men are.

Through following

God's intention has never been just to prod us from behind. His call to disciples is to "*follow* Me." In other words, God's Spirit desires to travel ahead of us, preparing the way so that we can safely follow in His footsteps. As we see how God is working in a particular situation, we need to fit ourselves into that situation and be sensitive to the Spirit's direction. If we choose not to follow God's leading, we will soon lose our sense of peace and can find ourselves disobeying the instructions we have received through God's Word or from pastors and leaders we look up to. Although we do not easily fall "in" or "out" of the Spirit of God, we can obey or disobey Him. As a friend of mine wisely used to comment about breaking the law of the land by speeding, "Up to seventy miles per hour the Lord is with you; over that you're on your own!"

Through Scripture

When we are following God's Word, we are on completely safe ground. God never changes His mind or contradicts His Word. As the psalmist said, "Your word is a lamp to my feet and a light for my path" (Ps. 119:105). Following Jesus must always involve obedience to the Spirit's Word in Scripture. Any claim to guidance that goes against the clear teachings of the Bible must be immediately rejected. If we think we are being led to have sex outside of marriage, for example, then the guidance has not come from the Spirit! We must always test our decisions by the teaching of Scripture.

Through people

This is another area in which we must proceed with caution. God's Spirit can lead us through other people, but He will only do so within the confines of His revealed Word in Scripture. Paul himself knew how to reject advice as well as receive it: "Through the Spirit, they urged Paul not to go on to Jerusalem. But when our time was up, we left and continued on our way" (Acts 21:4–5). However well-intentioned the advice may be, we must always assess its value before the Lord even if it is not against scriptural teaching (1 Thess. 5:19–21). Often when God intends to guide us into something, He will reveal it to more than one person—and confirm it for us as well!

A few years ago, I returned from a ministry trip to Sussex to be greeted by my wife with the words, "Darling, I think you should go to Israel." In all our years of marriage, she had never made such a suggestion. There was a personal desire at work here, because for many years I had wanted to visit the land of Israel, but in addition to the human reasons for her suggestion, Ruth firmly believed that this idea had originated with God.

Ruth contacted a friend of ours who frequently took parties to Israel, but he had no trips planned at that time. She also discovered that the cost for me to go alone would have been completely prohibitive. We were both in the process of dismissing the idea when, just three days later, a friend who had known nothing about this called me. He was convinced that the Lord wanted him to visit Israel in three weeks' time. He had never been to that country before, but the Lord had placed this conviction so firmly on his heart that he was not at liberty to ignore it! Having purchased his

35

ticket, he had felt equally constrained to buy one for me as well, although he knew nothing of my secret desire to go there.

The next day, I discovered that my engagements for the week in question had been suddenly canceled. When God intends something for His people, He brings it all together!

In dreams

God is not trying to hide His will from us. At times He will sometimes intervene while we are asleep. Paul experienced this: "During the night Paul had a vision of a man of Macedonia standing and begging him, 'Come over to Macedonia and help us!'" (Acts 16:9). Immediately he responded to God's call.

We must be careful to judge our dreams and visions correctly. They could be divinely or demonically inspired, although the latter is unusual for Christians. More likely, they are mere fantasies or the result of eating too much pizza the night before! We should not jump too quickly to the conclusion that God is telling us to do something in our dreams, especially if we have not been living in a close relationship with Him. But at times a dream may seem significant to us, and at that time it is a good idea to share it with other trustworthy Christians.

There are so many ways in which we can hear God: through inspired speech; the word of knowledge, word of wisdom, or prophecy; through the sense of agreement with others; or through a gentle nudge or a quiet inner conviction from the Spirit. Each way of hearing God does have one thing in common: they all require testing. The early church at Antioch provided the best example of receiving revelation: they gathered to fast and pray, and, in that context, the Holy Spirit spoke (Acts 13:2).

GOD WANTS US TO HEAR

Sometimes Christians become very worried about guidance, wondering if they have "missed God" somewhere. God does not want us to live in such fear. It is right for us to seek out God's way, but it is not right to be worried about it. God wants us to experience joy in finding His way—and we are more likely to do that if we commit to living right where we are and working on our relationship with Jesus. If we are doing that, we will be ready to hear God's voice when He wants us to move. If we start worrying about the next step too soon, we will start to imagine all sorts of things that aren't really there. Jesus reminds us, "Be concerned above everything else with the Kingdom of God and with what he requires of you. . . . Do not worry about tomorrow" (Matt. 6:33–34, GNT).

It is all too easy to become overly concerned with the details of God's plan for our lives and lose sight of His overall purpose. The most basic and wonderful truth is that God's chief purpose for us is to make us like Jesus. "Those whom God had already chosen he also set apart to become like his Son" (Rom. 8:29, GNT).

God never wants us to miss His way for us! Paul discovered that when he and his companions wanted to go to Bithynia against the will of God, "the Spirit of Jesus would not allow them to" (Acts 16:7). This indicates His loving commitment to us and His longing that we not go astray. However well-intentioned we may be, our mistaken notions of what is right often mean that the Holy Spirit must take action to prevent us from wandering in the wrong direction unintentionally.

It is not just the wrong place that God is concerned about, but also the wrong timing.

Mozambique is situated on the southeast coastline of Africa. Looking at a map, you may see it as a country that is far longer than it is wide; in fact, it looks like a long, thin stretch of land extending for hundreds of miles. On one occasion I was traveling north through Mozambique with some church leaders from the United States. We were all on a light aircraft piloted by two smartly dressed South Africans. At first impression, the pilots looked as if they knew where they were going—how wrong could they be?

We were traveling to a small, remote town called Chicualacuala, and before long we began to realize that our pilots were lost. This was confirmed when one of them turned around and blithely asked, "Does anyone know where the airstrip is? Or even the town?"

After an initial few moments of panic, we calmed down, but despite circling the area, we found that none of us could locate either the town or the landing strip. So, with fuel running low, we reluctantly turned back.

Our disappointment lay in the fact that Chicualacuala lay on the very edge of a famine-stricken area, and we knew that a large number of African pastors would have traveled long distances in their malnourished condition to meet with us. Some, we knew, had staked their very hopes on our visit. In their churches, adults and children alike were facing a bleak future without food. And they knew that our meeting might have been their last opportunity to share their plight with the world.

Still, there was nothing further we could do. At least we could console ourselves with the fact that the ground contingent would be in the town with the vehicles, awaiting our arrival. At least that was what we thought! At 2:45 A.M., there came a hammering at our door. It was bad news. The ground team had watched with dismay as we circled Chicualacuala, but then they had seen us fly away. They had similarly given up and made the eight-hour drive back to our base. Now we knew that even if we could get back to the village in the morning, the pastors would have left and gone home.

Yet I knew in my heart that we were meant to go there. Despite the reluctance of my colleagues and their unvoiced fears that it was my natural stubbornness rather than God's will that had taken over, we duly set off the next day. This time, we made sure we had directions to Chicualacuala!

Once we landed, we found that our arrival had not gone unnoticed! No less than half the town turned out to greet us; the local government official even had vehicles available for us to use!

After dividing the team in two and setting off in different directions, a few hours later we arrived in the village of Mapai. The pastor of the Assemblies of God church there was delighted to see us. He had been one of those who had made the long trek to Chicualacuala the day before and was overjoyed now to meet us. He guided us around the village so that we could see the little church and meet some of those who were now too weak to walk. We met little children with dreadfully thin arms and legs, but who had bloated stomachs and reddish-brown hair that is so often the hallmark of malnutrition.

The pastor showed us the food that was barely keeping them alive. Their meager diet consisted of dried worms and the wild fruit that elephants ate. Then we came across a man the pastor did not know. As we crouched on the ground beside him, we asked if he would tell us about himself, and he was happy to explain.

"I come from the village and left many years ago. I was a Christian then, but I went to Maputo [the capital city], and there I lost Jesus. Now I have finished with my life. So I came back to the village, and I am sitting beneath this tree and waiting to die. The reason I am not dead yet is that the people in the hut next to me had enough rice left for one more meal. After they had eaten it, there were still some grains of rice that had stuck to the side of the saucepan, and they gave it to me. Now I will die."

It was not difficult to discern that this was a divine appointment! Had we arrived at our planned destination the day before, we would only have met the pastors at a central location. We would never have been in this village, and the man himself had only just arrived. Kneeling there in the dust and dirt, the pastor and I had the joy of leading him back to Jesus.

This was not the end of the story. One of the church leaders with me was a businessman, and he immediately offered to pay for food for this man, for the church, and for the local churches in the area. In fact, on my next trip to Mozambique, I was excited to witness two pastors leaving to deliver the latest round of food supplies to the people in such desperate need. They were happy that we came back. Pastor Azarias of Chauque said, "They came in January, and now we see the fruit of that visit. We were dying because of hunger. Now we have fruit from the visitors. God will pay back to you, and He will bless all those who give. Because you are giving to Mozambique, God will bless you. We were eating roots before, but now we are eating maize given by our brothers, and we are happy."

I am constantly amazed at the way God always organizes things, for the timing and location of our entire visit had been divinely engineered to meet the needs of that man and of the entire community. The Lord will often place us in situations where we had no intention of going, and at a time that we least expect, to suit His divine purposes!

His desire is always that we might be able to achieve more through our lives than we would ever have dreamed of doing. This is possible because it is not us, but His Holy Spirit within us who is both doing the work and setting the direction. We may not know all of the results while we are here on earth, but one day heaven will be full of these delightful surprises for us.

The Holy Spirit is always at work to bring our lives into conformity with the will of God for us. He does this so that we may be able to cooperate actively with God's purposes through our lives. In a very real sense, guidance comes from the Holy Spirit in order that we might be the hands and feet of Jesus.

When God fences us in by creating major obstacles in our wandering path, these are actions of love to prevent us from hurting ourselves or damaging our lives. This was vividly illustrated in Hosea's relationship with his unfaithful wife, Gomer. God used their marriage to show in part how His people, Israel, had treated Him:

> Therefore I will block her path with thornbushes; I will wall her in so that she cannot find her way. She will chase after her lovers but not catch them; she will look for them but not find them. Then she will say, "I will go back to my husband as at first, for then I was better off than now."
>
> —HOSEA 2:6–7

Still, He leaves obedience as our response to His grace.

GOD IS AT WORK IN US!

How does all this happen? Jesus never stops working within our lives. Through His Holy Spirit, He is working to teach us what it means to live in God's world God's way.

In fact, Jesus told His disciples that they would actually be better off without Him: "But I tell you the truth: It is for your good that I am going away. Unless I go away, the Counselor will not come to you" (John 16:7). Impossible as it may seem for all of us who would love to have physically walked and talked by the shores of Galilee with Jesus, He said that those of us who live today are in a superior position! Because He ascended to the Father, we do not merely have God walking beside us but living within us!

No Christian should ever regard him or herself as at the mercy of a vicious, fallen world. Unlike the rabbit who was trapped by forces beyond its control, we have been provided with the finest Guide this world has ever known—the Holy Spirit—God Himself.

6

ENEMY AT WORK

She was so excited—really thrilled. The victory had been so sudden and totally overwhelming. God had intervened in such an amazing and unexpected way, and God had used her more than she had ever dreamed possible.

And then, just as suddenly, it was over. She was alone and very tired. Would things ever be the same again? Had God come on the scene, only to leave her all alone in the end? Her moment of highest achievement had come—and gone. Perhaps it was inevitable that just at that moment, temptation struck. Sometimes it is too easy to forget that we have an enemy at work—and he is against us.

Elijah would have sympathized. He went through the same kind of experience until he was rescued by the still, quiet voice of the Spirit of God. After his moment of greatest triumph at the top of Mount Carmel in which God used him mightily to judge the prophets of Baal, he found himself running for his life, fleeing to escape the clutches of an evil queen. So unaware was he of the potential for divine intervention in his situation that he even contemplated suicide.

There is nothing unusual about this particular sequence of events. It even happened to Jesus. After thirty years in total obscurity, Jesus emerged from Nazareth, just about the most unlikely place imaginable. He was publicly baptized by John, and at that moment God the Father spoke from heaven to endorse His Son. But directly after that point of triumph, after having been vindicated before His fellow countrymen, the Holy Spirit immediately drove Jesus into the desert to be tempted by the enemy. Tired, hungry, and alone, Jesus faced Satan himself. But the Holy Spirit had placed Him in that position for a reason!

Why does God follow such a pattern? Is this the way God repays faithful service? Yes, in a way, it is. After all, Jesus warned us that if we are faithful in small things, we will be trusted with bigger matters. So often we view temptation as entirely a negative event. But in many cases, that conclusion would be far from the truth. Satan will always view temptation as an opportunity to score, but time and again, God is simply waiting to reverse our moment of potential tragedy and turn it into one of triumph. At these times, Satan may choose the moment when he believes we are most vulnerable, but God uses it to strengthen and equip us for our Christian life and witness—checkmate!

THE DESERT

The three years of ministry that lay ahead of Jesus were to be the most crucial years in the history of humankind. After this period of time, the world would never be the same again. It was the task of the Holy Spirit to be Jesus' teacher, to prepare Him for His life of ministry. In exactly the same way, Jesus promised that "the Counselor, the Holy Spirit, whom the Father will send in my name, will teach you all things" (John 14:26). But because a teacher needs a classroom, the Holy Spirit sent Jesus to His traditional training ground—the desert.

It was in the wilderness that the Holy Spirit taught Israel. The desert was also the training ground for John the Baptist, who fulfilled his training so well that Jesus testified of him: "I tell you, among those born of women there is no one greater than John" (Luke 7:28).

The road to spiritual maturity is not an easy one. Frequently it lies through what many have termed a "wilderness experience," and at these times when we are tired and alone, and we feel as if we have lost touch with God, Satan sees and seizes his opportunity.

Jesus knew the temptation would come, and He fasted to prepare Himself for the conflict. As He was later to emphasize, some battles cannot be won without just that kind of preparation. The Christian life has never been a glib exercise in "easy-believism," but it is and always has been a clear-cut struggle with no less an opponent than the enemy of our souls, Satan himself.

In this serious exercise of spiritual warfare, it is of vital importance to note that we are engaged in a battle not just against wrong thoughts or habits, but against an actual, personal enemy who represents spiritual reality at its very worst.

For this reason, Satan should never be dismissed as an irrational fear or a joke. He is dangerous, and in that regard he must be treated with respect. But on the other hand, he is not all-powerful, and we do not need to fear him. Scripture is quite insistent that although there is a very real devil, he cannot compare for a single moment with God Himself. Satan is a strong and persuasive opponent, but he has already been conquered. The victory over this enemy has already been won on our behalf!

Throughout the history of the church, there have always been individuals who have known the reality of these truths and put them into practice. During the Reformation in the sixteenth century, Martin Luther sensed that he was involved in a close encounter with Satan himself, and he ended up throwing an inkwell at the enemy!

In the twentieth century, the great Pentecostal evangelist and church-planter Smith Wigglesworth was disturbed from his sleep at around four o'clock one morning. He woke to find Satan standing at the foot of his bed. Despite being both startled and surprised, he managed to make a truly biblically and theologically correct response. He simply said, "Oh, it's you," and turned over and went back to sleep.

He could do this because he knew that because he had inherited a new life in Christ Jesus, he had nothing to fear! His only task was to obey the Father and seek to do His will.

This point is made no less than 366 times in the Bible, where we are repeatedly given the instruction and reassurance, "Don't be afraid!" Why are these comforting words repeated so often? Once for every day of the year and an extra one for leap year! It is absolutely essential that we take hold of this truth.

Undoubtedly most of us are slow learners. We do not usually learn these truths automatically. Many of us regard a "desert experience" as something negative, a period in which we primarily concentrate on survival. But often, as it was for Jesus, the desert is God's schoolroom in which He prepares us for all that lies ahead. It is not when life is easy but when we are going through difficult times that God will often choose to speak directly to us. It is when we are enduring an arid wilderness experience that God demonstrates to us His victory over the enemy.

If Satan had won his conflict with Jesus in the wilderness, then God's plan of redemption would have failed. Thank God, this did not happen because, led by the Spirit, Jesus was ready. And once the conflict was successfully over, angels were ready to assist the Son of God to make a swift and total recovery. In boxing terms, it had been victory by a first-round knockout, but the gymnasium in which to prepare for the fight, as well as the arena itself, was the desert.

THE DEVIL

Some Christians manage to live most of their spiritual lives in blissful ignorance of the devil's very existence. Because they never trouble him, he rarely bothers them!

The very idea of a personal devil is enough to cause many to break out into guffaws of laughter. Yet these very same folks find nothing strange in accepting the necessity for avoiding ladders, knocking on wood, or even "kissing the Blarney Stone." Notions of devouring alien monsters, ancient curses that have retained their virulent potency, and even extraterrestrial beings enjoying a brief excursion to Planet Earth are all regarded as perfectly possible. But the concept of a personalized demonic architect of evil—Satan himself? No way!

DESCENDING LIKE A DOVE

It seems to me that as human beings we are becoming very selective in our acceptance of the supernatural. I am originally from Britain, a nation whose religious origins lie in the sphere of witchcraft. For Christians there, Halloween is no laughing matter. Its origins lay in "All Saint's Eve," a church festival that had emerged in reaction against early pagan practices of providing sacrifices and gifts to appease demon spirits. Every Halloween I would debate with real-life witches on national radio or television. Imagine my surprise upon coming to America to find that Halloween has become so sanitized—even among Christians—that some church halls are even used for Halloween parties! It was quite a shock to see that Halloween in the U.S. is seen as little more than harmless fun.

Most of us are quite happy with whatever falls within our comfort zones or can provide us with entertainment. To contemplate the existence of a devil who has his own personality and possesses the power to invade ours as well is, for most people today, quite out of the question. This is easy to understand when we consider that the whole concept of Satan conflicts with the basic presuppositions of our contemporary world-view. How can a materialistic world accept the existence of a nonmaterial being?

How can a "rational" world accept the existence of a force that is only acknowledged by what is perceived as a lunatic fringe of Satanists or devil-worshipers?

How can "evil" be spoken of when we reject its existence?

The simple fact remains that the very idea of Satan does not agree with a twenty-first-century mind-set. The age of hedonism is alive and well and living among us. Our postmodern world has decided that everything is there to be enjoyed. We may acknowledge some inconsistency in our fascination with the paranormal, but because we hate to admit the possibility that we could be wrong, everything "interesting" is left in, while ideas of God and Satan, good and evil, are left firmly locked out.

C. S. Lewis once perceptively observed, "There are two equal and opposite errors into which our race can fall about devils. One is to disbelieve their existence. The other is to believe and to feel an unhealthy interest in them. They themselves are equally pleased by both errors and hail a materialist or a magician with the same delight."[1]

When we begin to be totally committed to God and to living in the power of the Holy Spirit, that is the moment when Satan starts to worry! He fears being exposed to the light. He far prefers the darkness and the protection it gives him. He fears those who might wake up and stand against him. The plain and simple fact is that he is really a coward at heart.

These statements may sound surprising, but in reality, Satan has very limited power and personality when compared with that of the Holy Spirit.

The devil is a defeated opponent.

First of all, Satan is only a created being. He is in no way divine, and he demonstrates this by using violence, lies, and deception to achieve his objectives. The devil is a liar, a deceiver, and one who gets it wrong! Nowhere is this more clearly illustrated than when the devil stared ultimate defeat in the face—and he panicked. Two thousand years ago, Satan observed a situation that he had always dreaded occurring. God's Son was bringing salvation and freedom to ordinary men and women, and Satan could not tolerate it. He set out to frustrate God's purposes, but instead he ended up doing the very things necessary to accomplish them!

Satan engineered the crucifixion of Jesus. As Jesus hung there, nailed to a cross, Satan was convinced that he had rid himself of the one man who had dared to live in the full power and authority of the Holy Spirit. But three days later, God, through that same Holy Spirit, mightily resurrected Jesus from the grave and restored Him to His side. The created world looked on in amazement. Who had ever heard of a God who would suffer, let alone die, for His own creation? Within days, there were 120, then 3,000, then an uncountable number whose lives had been filled with the Holy Spirit and who were living in the way that God had always intended for them to live.

Satan has a major disadvantage in his struggle against God.

His pride causes him to try to compete in the wrong league. He is only a created being who was expelled from heaven for seeking to oppose God. As such he can never be a true opponent of the Holy Spirit. What is more, Satan ultimately knows this—and fears it! Throughout the centuries, many outstanding Christians have recognized this fact. It is only because there are so many of us who have either ignored or rejected this truth that the devil has gotten away with as much as he has!

Satan is limited by time and space.

He can only be in one place at a time. The Holy Spirit, on the other hand, can be everywhere in the same instant. Satan is terribly limited and must employ an army of demon spirits to move at his command. For this reason, we are very unlikely to have a personal encounter with Satan himself. His activities are both temporary and localized. What a contrast to the Holy Spirit who lives *inside* the people of God all day long! And on the exceptionally rare occurrence when Satan might come to trouble us in person, we should rejoice as it would mean that we were saving all our brothers and sisters throughout the world from having a problem with him at that moment!

Satan's bitterness and anger are so fierce that he has engaged in violent actions against those who have given the direction of their lives to the Holy Spirit.

Ultimately he would love to kill us outright, but recognizing that this lies beyond his powers, Satan has instead chosen to distract many of us from our purpose in this world. He tries to hang us up on inessentials so that we spend hours arguing about issues that have no direct impact on how we live, rather than get on with the business of serving Jesus in His world. Through every means possible Satan tries to make us see the Holy Spirit as a cause of division rather than unity. The devil's strategy is often brilliantly simple. He tries to make us feel either arrogant because of an "experience" we had or inferior because we did not have it!

How easy it is to fall for Satan's deception! Our spiritual insecurities can make us far too easy a prey. We can be so afraid that others are ahead of us in the race that instead of rejoicing at the way God leads them, we insist that they come back to join us on our own spiritual pathway.

In the New Testament, the Greek word for Satan, *satanas*, only rarely carries the meaning of our "opponent." This is because Jesus is the victor. It is by His Spirit that we triumph over Satan, and because he knows this, he rarely dares to stand against us. More frequently the word means "accuser."

As a defeated foe, Satan is like the Mafia boss who continues to run his operation from prison. Or like Osama bin Laden, who is condemned by most of world opinion as the murderer of hundreds and hundreds of people. But the fact is that he never met any of them, nor would he have personally been known to many of the perpetrators. Yet through networks of cells that he inspired and a few angry men whom he equipped with the means to commit awful atrocities, the evil of this one single man has changed the world. This is only a man. Imagine how much the devil has achieved through instruments like this one because he hides behind the evil that men do while remaining the true source of all of it.

The devil is not engaged in flamboyant actions. Often he is content with simply whispering words in our ears in order to create doubt in our minds about God. Once he causes us to question the power and activity of the Holy Spirit in our lives, it is only a short leap to make us doubt whether or not we really are Christian.

There is no reason to ask where such reactions come from. They are from the enemy!

However, just because Satan has been defeated does not mean that he cannot still prove to be annoying! His constant irritations merely prove that, from his point of view, we are actually worth bothering! If that were not the case, he would leave us alone.

This does not mean, though, that we can get away with placing all the blame on him for our own weaknesses and failures. So often we use the lame excuse, "The devil made me do it." He didn't—we gave in to temptation and need forgiveness, not self-justification! Sometimes I think that if the devil were actually guilty of half the things of which he has been accused, then he would be a very happy devil indeed! But it would be worse if Jesus were only half the Victor we claim Him to be—and that could never be the case.

This is why Jesus taught His disciples to pray that they would not fall into temptation, that they would be preserved against the onslaughts of the evil one. He did so because He won the first skirmish with the enemy in the wilderness and the ultimate victory on the cross. Through the triumph of crucified love, He inaugurated a wonderful new life through His death. This once-and-for-all sacrifice was the turning point in history, as the power of darkness was forever exterminated in the light of an empty tomb.

A new era had dawned, and the day of the Holy Spirit had arrived. Now the possibility of life in a new dimension had become a vivid reality.

7

TRIAL OF STRENGTH

I never anticipated the reception that I was to receive at one village in Mozambique. Frankly, I was a little embarrassed to receive a hero's welcome upon entering a village that I had never visited before. It was only when the tribal elders explained that it was Mozambican women on my staff who had earned this honor for me that I began to understand. The more questions I asked, the more the story began to unfold.

For you to fully appreciate the situation I was in, I must first share a little about the pagan and cultural heritage of this tribe. An African nurse on our staff, Linda, had begun to operate a "child survival" program for World Relief in that part of the country. When she visited this particular village, she discovered the high percentage of children under five years of age who were dying from diarrhea. The people simply accepted this as a fact of life. It was a problem that had been with them for decades. Whenever a child fell sick, the family followed the instructions of the witchdoctors.

A bowl of water would be placed outside the family's hut, and a damp cloth would be used to wipe the child's bottom. Afterward, the cloth was placed in the bowl of water. After each bout of diarrhea, the process would be repeated. Every night a portion of the water from the bowl was carefully measured out, diluted, and then given to the child to drink. The bowl of water was retained overnight, and the next morning this routine would continue.

Eventually the baby or young child was forced to drink barely diluted diarrhea. The inevitable result was that many of them died.

Linda became quite desperate because this practice had traditionally received the backing of the tribal elders. Few would have dared to defy the witchdoctors' instructions. Patiently Linda worked to convince the village mothers that what they were doing was wrong and unhealthy. Eventually she succeeded; the bowl of diarrhea was replaced with a simple salt solution, and the children began to survive. Because of this, the power and influence of the witchdoctors were undermined and diminished, and the people became far more open to other spiritual answers.

Perhaps it is not surprising that today we have nearly 25,000 fifteen- to twenty-five-year-old Mozambican young people from that area who are meeting in weekly Bible studies to learn more about loving and serving Jesus Christ.

Even still, the question remains: Who on earth would have originated such a vile, evil way of "curing" young children? Was it purely ignorance, or did more malevolent forces play a part in creating this tragedy?

THE DECISIVE FACTOR

Sadly, many of us are strangely ignorant when it comes to issues relating to the reality of the Holy Spirit. As I have already pointed out, it is a sad fact that throughout the history of the church, theologians have been less confident in talking about God the Holy Spirit than about the Father or the Son. Controversy has often dogged the activities of the Holy Spirit. Continually people have objected to claims of His activity by responding that God cannot work in this way or the other. Certainly we feel safer with the activities of God the Father, revealed in creation, or the Son as we see Him in Jesus. The dominant activities of the Holy Spirit lie in the here and now, and those can seem far more dangerous. It is safer to look into the past than to experience God's power in our lives in the present!

Jesus promised His disciples that they would not have to struggle on in their own strength. "I will not leave you as orphans; I will come to you" (John 14:18). Our major difficulty is that each of us is incapable of living the life of God without the power of the Holy Spirit. As Paul said, "For I have the desire to do what is good, but I cannot carry it out" (Rom. 7:18). But God has not abandoned us to this problem! He has not left us to struggle on, somehow trying to survive alone. Rather than being neglected orphans, we are the proud possessors of God's Spirit. This Spirit is the Holy Spirit, who expects us to be holy, too, and He works in our lives to bring that about. But our response will inevitably bring down upon us the direct opposition of Satan himself.

Jesus could only face life on earth in opposition to the will of Satan through the Holy Spirit. As soon as Jesus was baptized, the Holy Spirit filled Him. "He saw the Spirit of God descending like a dove and lighting on him" (Matt. 3:16).

F. B. Meyer, that great evangelical preacher of the early twentieth century, reminded his listeners that they should "never forget that our Lord's ministry was not in the power of the second Person of the blessed Trinity but in the power of the third Person."[1] Similarly, in a new century, we need to remember that same lesson.

THE DILEMMA: TURN STONES INTO BREAD

Of the three direct challenges that Jesus received from Satan, this must have seemed the most straightforward. Scripture states simply that after a forty-day fast, "he [Jesus] was hungry" (Luke 4:2). Most of us would have been as well!

Satan is a specialist in the field of easy answers, and he offered a very simple solution. He knew that even if the only thing Jesus did was turn the stones into bread, He would have misused His divine power to alleviate His own hunger.

A few weeks later, Jesus was to feed crowds of four and five thousand with a few loaves and fish. All He had to do was to advance God's own basic strategy by a matter of weeks, and Jesus could satisfy His own physical needs. Time and again, it is at this level of self-interest that Satan will strike. He will offer anything to keep us complacent and self-indulgent. He will tell us, "Satisfy yourself; enjoy your meetings, books, conferences, teaching tapes, and friends—just don't exercise spiritual concern for others. Save it all for yourself. Don't waste your time on the needs of those around you, but concentrate on number one." This temptation could even include the desire to satisfy our own spiritual needs, even our own desire to be holy. Anything seems to be acceptable to Satan if it means that we are content to leave him alone within his own dominion.

Now this is directly opposed to those concerns that are prompted by the Holy Spirit. He wants to mobilize us to reach out from our spiritual ghettos into a dying world. Satan, on the other hand, desperately wants to keep us fat, self-interested, relatively content, and at home!

That is why the devil is not overly concerned about our abstaining from certain sinful appetites. Of course these are important. Personal holiness must always be a major issue for Christian believers, but it should never come at the expense of ignoring social injustice and the pain of others in our world. While we concentrate on avoiding relatively minor pitfalls, we live in a world that is missing out on the message of Jesus.

THE DANGER: CHEAP GAINS

Satan's offers of help are usually attractive, and his second temptation of Jesus was no exception. Satan offered Jesus the divine legacy of the kingdoms of the world—but without the pain of the cross. All Jesus had to do was to worship His enemy.

The temptation here is to follow an easy pathway. Satan's gift to Jesus would only, at best, have been temporary. God's legacy to His obedient Son was to be eternal. In exactly the same way, we must choose between our own short-lived ambitions and the direction that God has prepared for our lives.

Such commitment may seem strange to others in society. I remember the occasion when God told a local church leader to sell his private house and move to a place where church contacts and influence were few and far between. His colleagues found it difficult to understand, but following the living God can usually be expected to be neither easy nor cheap. As Christians, we are faced with a simple choice of bowing the knee to Satan for short-term gain or looking to Jesus for an eternal inheritance.

This may involve the inconvenience of moving to a less desirable part of the world. It could mean changing jobs or even facing suffering, persecution, or both! But as A. W. Tozer aptly put it, "We can afford to suffer now; we'll have a long eternity to enjoy ourselves!"[2] The Holy Spirit has been given to lead us into truth. It is to His direction that we must turn if we are to follow God's way for our lives, for we can never succeed on our own.

THE DECEPTION: DESTROY YOURSELF!

Satan is a master at quoting the Bible out of context. He offered Jesus a shortcut to avoid the cross, an easy route leading to instant popularity. "Throw Yourself down," he said. "God's angels will catch You!" How well he knew that the promise was conditional, based on Jesus' actions being in the will of God. How he longed for the body of Jesus to be smashed onto the rocks below.

Step outside of the will of God, and disaster is the result. Satan's arguments can be clever, for he is a better theologian than any of us—but he remains the devil.

Jesus used two weapons to secure His victory over this temptation. He stood firmly on the Scriptures, and He operated in the power of the Holy Spirit. He repeated back to Satan the phrase, "It is written," trusting the Word of God that proceeds from the Holy Spirit (Acts 1:16; 28:25).

As we spend time reading God's Word, the Holy Spirit leads us not only to understand the truth but also to live the truth. The Holy Spirit cannot tolerate sin, and His power is available to keep us separate from Satan's superficial offers. In Romans 1:4, Paul called Him the "Spirit of holiness." He is the One God has placed within us in order that we may stand and grow in Him. "God is faithful; he will not let you be tempted beyond what you can bear.

But when you are tempted, he will also provide a way out so that you can stand up under it" (1 Cor. 10:13).

What is the Holy Spirit seeking to achieve? He often allows the devil to overreach himself by taking the struggles he brings us and using them to fulfill His own supreme purposes. The unavoidable conclusion is that God allows us to be tempted in order that He may cause our lives to more perfectly reflect the love and character of His Son. His ultimate intent is that each of us might daily more clearly resemble Jesus.

When the Holy Spirit observes areas of weakness in our lives, He acts in the same manner as a Peruvian potter. The potter flicks the rim of a pot and listens for the ring that proclaims a perfect glaze. If the sound is wrong, he places the pot back in the oven until the fire has done its work. Only when the tone is perfect is the pot approved for use.

In our own lives, God will highlight our areas of weakness. In the wilderness, God searched throughout Israel for holiness and right living among His people. Instead of yielding to God's authority and receiving His aid, they failed in their response to temptation, again and again. For this reason, after crossing the Red Sea, it took them forty years to complete a fortnight's journey. God longed to take them into the Promised Land, but the majority of them ended up as bleached bones in the desert.

It can be exactly the same for us. Temptation itself is not sin. God can use it to mold our lives, but our failure to respond can send us back over the same ground for lap after lap until we finally surrender to His love and authority in our lives. The Holy Spirit will not be content until all those hardened areas of failure within us, those long-continued weaknesses, have been changed by His love and power.

BETTER LUCK NEXT TIME

"When the devil had finished all this tempting, he left him until an opportune time" (Luke 4:13). By leading Him into the wilderness, the Holy Spirit had initiated a vital process in the life of Jesus. An ongoing narrative of victory over Satan had been established, and the anointing of the Spirit at His baptism had proven to be real. Jesus entered the wilderness "full of the Holy Spirit" (v. 1). Triumphing over Satan, He "returned to Galilee in the power of the Spirit" (v. 14). It was His being full of the Spirit that led to His power. The result was a defeated Satan, and the years of triumph had begun.

Even in the Garden of Gethsemane, temptation to take an easier way would not divert or deflect Jesus from His God-ordained path. The writer of Hebrews parallels the way Jesus was tempted to the temptations that each one of us is called to endure. There is just one difference, for in this three-round contest, Jesus went the entire distance and did not lose a single round of the fight. He endured everything, and yet, He never sinned (Heb. 4:15).

But we too will face temptations that may certainly parallel those endured by Jesus. These can be summarized as the temptation to whine (to bemoan our physical condition), to shine (to be content with our superficial popularity or acceptance), or to recline (to take the easy way out). None of these options are good enough for God. They were not good enough for Jesus, and they should not be good enough for us.

Jesus gained the victory alone, so that we don't have to. He Himself gives us the strength with which to win the battle. Because Jesus has been completely victorious on the cross and because we too know that same Holy Spirit, there is an inescapable conclusion. When we live in obedience to the will of Jesus for our lives and have the power of His Spirit within us, we too can enjoy victory over the powers and the deceptions of the devil.

8

A WORLD WITHOUT
ANSWERS

All around the world there are particular countries that have managed either to attract or to repel their wealthier neighbors—and with significant results.

Haiti is a good case in point. Only thirty years ago, when compared to the neighboring Dominican Republic, Haiti's future looked bright. Today that has changed. Her once burgeoning tourist industry has collapsed in ruins, and whole sections of her economy appear to be shattered. Occasionally attempts at change are made, but any claims that Haiti is a budding and emergent democracy are met with skepticism. Corruption rules Haiti as solidly as ever. It is not safe to walk the streets alone by night, and it can even be dangerous in the daytime. When my youngest daughter, Suzy, was fifteen, as she was being driven along the streets of Port-au-Prince, her vehicle passed a man who had just been murdered. It was in the middle of the day!

If you fly across the island, the boundary line between Haiti and the Dominican Republic becomes obvious. The trees on the Haitian side of the border have been indiscriminately felled, and only scrubland remains. Haiti's poverty stands in stark contrast to the Dominican Republic's greater political stability, thriving tourist industry, developing economy, and lush trees and foliage!

As I walked out of filming a section of one of Haiti's quasi-voodoo ceremonies (designed only for the more adventurous tourist with a hunger for the bizarre side of life), I felt repelled by what I had just witnessed. The feelings of disgust did not come because I was a "mature" Westerner who realized that what I had seen was a fake. Instead I was nauseated because what I had seen was a shadow of those powers that have dominated Haiti for so long.

The camera crew followed me as I made my way toward one of Haiti's largest churches. They filmed me as I stood outside, explaining that because I was from England, I came from a country that also had witchcraft in its history. I certainly had no difficulty believing in the existence of the devil, but like a former voodoo priest whom we also interviewed, I am even firmer in my conviction in Satan's downfall!

BATTLE ROYALE!

In my mind, there is absolutely no doubt that when darkness suddenly descended upon a crude Roman cross outside of Jerusalem some two thousand years ago, the death of Jesus changed the course of world history.

The amazing truth is that as Satan gazed upon the earth in that moment, he saw one solitary individual who had lived a life totally filled in every part by the Holy Spirit—but who was now dead. As he breathed a sigh of relief at the sight of the Son of God hanging upon a cross, he could scarcely have realized that within a few short weeks, that one man would have commissioned the beginnings of a mighty army.

But Satan didn't realize what was actually taking place. Those moments when darkness fell witnessed the Son of God on a cross as He chose to surrender His life. The result was that His sacrifice would usher in the dawn of a whole new era in human experience. Within three short days, the grave was empty, and a dead man was making a surprise appearance to His astounded followers! Only six weeks later, in the upper room, the Holy Spirit arrived in tongues of flame.

His dramatic entrance initiated the disciples of Jesus with the power to change their world. From this moment on, He would come to live with all those ordinary men and women who surrendered themselves to Jesus Christ, and He would remain with them as an indwelling power transforming their lives both now and for eternity.

None of this could ever have been possible apart from the cross. Only there could divine forgiveness meet the requirements of divine holiness. On the cross, heaven's love and justice met—and embraced. Now the Spirit would come to forgiven lives. Now God's purposes would be fulfilled among the Gentiles. Now the church would emerge as a covenant people of God. Now the good news of saving faith in Jesus would spread throughout the earth. Motivated by His love for humankind and supremely by His desire to do His Father's will, Jesus paid the price for our sins. He died on the cross out of love for us, and this single event clearly and finally initiated Satan's downfall. Now no one can ever doubt this one single and gloriously liberating truth: our enemy has been defeated!

IGNORANCE OF THE DEVIL

The real problem for Haiti did not ultimately lie in its form of government, its economy, its corruption, its incipient violence, or anything else. As other countries rejected Haitian pleas for help for these more superficial reasons, they were actually missing the point. These were only symptoms of the underlying problem, for the spiritual darkness that fills Haiti pervades every area of its national life. That is why the Haitian churches have begun to take action against the history of voodoo that has permeated their society.

How do we begin to convince a world that is so totally obsessed by materialism and the physical realm that there really is another dimension to life? How do we explain that spiritual powers can often be the invisible pianist playing upon a clearly visible piano?

Within the Western world, we find ourselves living in a society that believes something can only exist if it can be heard, touched, tasted, seen, or smelled. We live in the aftermath of a nineteenth- and twentieth-century materialistic world-view that placed an enormous emphasis on scientific and technological development. Men like Benjamin Franklin developed this view from the optimistic assumption that modern man was very different from the predecessors from whom he had evolved, and he would very shortly "come of age" and institute a glorious "brave new world." Great stress was placed on exercising tolerance, reason, and strictly human common sense to ultimately fulfill our potential.

The idea was that "God," if indeed one had ever existed, had created the world as an elaborate mechanical device. He had wound it up once like a giant clockwork toy, and then He excused Himself to go off to other activities, leaving this world to fend for itself. Our tiny universe was now little more than a totally independent and closed entity, locked off from a God who was no longer concerned with the affairs of humankind.

With these assumptions, it is no wonder materialism became the rule of the day. If God had effectively left this world, then the possibility of supernatural intervention in the affairs of this world had departed with Him. He could only be replaced by self-reliance. In His absence, the inevitable conclusion is that humankind alone represents the only real hope for the future. Only the present material world was viewed as having reality. There could be no divine, miraculous, or supernatural forces in the universe. Forces that defied human explanation were still recognized but not believed to be supernatural in origin.

Such views prevailed throughout the first half of the twentieth century, and then popular support for this perspective began to wane. The problem was that after two World Wars, the origination of the atomic bomb, starvation on a worldwide scale, and a raging AIDS epidemic of global proportions, belief in man as the "measure of all things" had begun to look like a hollow sham.

INTRODUCING A COUNTERFEIT FAITH

Pessimism and despair had replaced the mood of optimism. A new faith was needed to stand in the gap. But instead of a return to Christian truth and the living God, the growing and genuine hunger for spiritual realities and fulfillment resulted in an incredible growth in astrology, Eastern religions, new cults, occultism, and transcendental meditation. Just a few years ago, most people would have dismissed all of these as crude, simplistic, and infantile. Now this odd "smorgasbord" of quasi-religious experimental practices is dignified by the name "New Age" and has become the fresh faith for millions of people. So "reason" is now out, and "experience" is back in, the only difference being that now the experience no longer has to be reasonable!

A fascination with occultism, including its potential entertainment value, has begun both to occupy and consume the minds of many people. Nowhere is this more evident than among children. Some estimate that over 70 percent of teenagers in Western Europe have experimented with Ouija boards, levitation, or séances.

The concept of "power" was understood by both ancient and more primitive contemporary cultures as representing the coming together of spiritual and material factors. Within the Western world, over the last few hundred years, the notion of "power" has been related to material power. It has become completely unfashionable to consider that spirits, gods, or demons could in any way be regarded as the agents behind events in our world. We now confidently assume that when ancient civilizations talked of gods, spirits, or powers, their ideas were rooted in ignorance, psychological factors, mass hallucinations, or simply lack of proper medical knowledge. Our preference today is for a more rational approach based upon the physical laws of the universe as revealed by modern science.

The result of this is that any sense of need for a personal God has been reduced to a level that is neither real nor relevant, let alone desirable. It has become generally accepted that a consistent advance in scientific understanding will eventually meet all the needs of modern society. Modern man has become a quintessentially self-reliant being—or for the moment he may think that is the case!

THE "GODS" OF OUR AGE

It seemed that materialism had fixed a rigid boundary between the Creator and His creation. Technological growth had provided confirmation for most people that God is no longer necessary for life in a modern world. After all, who needs a healer, even a miracle worker, when there is a hospital just down the road?

As we unconsciously passed from a "modernist" era and entered a "postmodern" world, we moved from a conviction that truth was absolute to a fresh realization that each of us could depend on our own perspective. Therefore, the role of experience and phenomena came to be more acceptable than it had been before.

More and more we have found that while many believe that there are no divine or supernatural forces at work in the universe, we have been forced to concede that there are many things we do not understand. Many events and circumstances simply defy human explanation. It is easy to affirm that when a car breaks down, it is more likely due to a mechanical fault than a mischievous demon needing to be cast out of the machinery. However, the results of a private séance or the exercise of astral projection often lie outside the realm of rational explanation. The same applies to overseas phenomena such as the practice of voodoo in Haiti and activities associated with the spirit world in African tribal religions. A "rational" person may consider these "powers" to be the product of simple people's imagination. Many modern and "rational" societies may relegate these concepts to the level of myths but demonstrate their own fascination with the unknown. Contemporary France, for example, the epitome of a modern materialistic society, today has more psychic mediums than priests.[1]

Deprived of "absolute truth," our lives have become full of unanswered questions. These tend to include problem areas such as:

- What follows death?
- Why do each tribe and culture select something or someone to worship?
- From where does our human creativity emerge?
- Why do I have an inner personal desire to uncover the transcendent, to find something "out there"?

Such questions all defy our desire for easy answers. As a result, the French philosopher Blaise Pascal concluded that "reason's last step is the recognition that there is an infinite number of things which are beyond it. It is merely feeble if it does not go as far as to realize that."[2]

We are all still struggling to recognize the fact that God has come to our world—as a Person—to reveal His reality to us! And one reason for His coming is to remove the threat of an enemy who is still at work in the world today.

9

DANGER—POWERS AT PLAY

So many unanswered questions and unexplained mysteries
have left gaps in our understanding, and fantasy and supersti-
tion have been allowed to complement what was already a
thoroughly corrupt picture.

Steven Spielberg found a winning formula when he directed
films in which action-packed scenes were placed in a fantasy
framework. He made his fortune from the Indiana Jones trilogy in
which supernatural powers constantly intruded into the adven-
ture. No rational explanation was offered as to the power of the
Holy Grail, an idol temple, or the awesome concentration of spiritual energy in the fictitious ark of the covenant, and that alone
produced a sense of fascination. Yet the way in which these were
so closely related to real situations was cleverly designed to
heighten the sense of intrigue. It took the story out of the realm of
science fiction and into a realm of possibility if certain "powers"
were real. At the same time, each was designed to so radically defy
natural reason that they kept viewers firmly convinced that it was
only the product of a vivid imagination.

As one contemporary author has concluded:

> Angels, spirits, principalities, powers, gods, Satan—these,
> along with all other spiritual realities, are unmentionables
> of our culture. The dominant materialistic worldview has
> absolutely no place for them. These archaic relics of a

superstitious past are unspeakable because modern secularism has massive resistance even to thinking about these phenomena, having fought so long and hard to rid itself of every vestige of transcendence.[1]

FORCES WE TRY TO IGNORE

Today there are over 500 million people who follow various forms of primal religion.[2] These people view the world as being populated by invisible powers that permeate the whole of human life and existence. These unseen powers are frequently seen to attach themselves to ancestors, mythological heroes, inanimate objects such as trees and flowers, or even the wider forces of nature. A concern for personal welfare and for the well-being of the community means that such "forces" must be kept happy. They confer personal safety, success, and failure, so they must be constantly appeased.

The use of magic and ritual, usually facilitated by specialists such as pagan priests or witchdoctors, becomes an essential part of life for the followers of these ideas. Only by such means can protection be achieved against the mischievous activities of malevolent spirits. It is easy to joke about such beliefs, but their influence remains strong in many societies—and with strongly negative results.

Some of the stories in this book only make sense when viewed against this background. Pagan practices have exercised an incredible influence over so many people, and still do today.

THE BIBLE'S PERSPECTIVE

The Bible clearly disagrees with the conclusions of human reason. Rather than adopting the "either . . . or" mentality with regard to materialism and primal religions, the Bible chooses to adopt a "both . . . and" understanding. It speaks of the powers in a variety of ways. They can be both:

■ Heavenly and earthly
■ Human and divine

Danger—Powers at Play

- Spiritual and political
- Invisible and structural

This is why the whole concept of the powers is so difficult to understand. Because we cannot devise a neat little box in which to place them, we can be guilty of ignoring them. The Bible does not present us with tidy distinctions in relation to unseen spirits. Scripture does not teach that demons only cause sickness and should only be treated by physicians and psychiatrists. Nor does it suggest that principalities and powers are merely sociopolitical structures and should be the sole concern of politicians, economists, and sociologists. Instead, Scripture sees the physical and spiritual as intermingled, and it presents us with many vivid pictures of forces at work in our world—forces clearly beyond our human control.

That is the reason why sickness may be (and usually is) a purely physical ailment, but we cannot put it past the enemy to use sickness to attack us. In the same way, biblical "powers" will usually refer to actual human agencies such as social systems, secular authorities, and political structures. Yet these physical institutions will have spiritual forces acting as controlling influences upon them. (See Matthew 20:25; Mark 10:42; Luke 22:25; Acts 4:26.)

These forces are not merely powerful. The Bible often calls them names such as *principalities*, *powers*, and *thrones*, and they clearly refer to superhuman powers (Rom. 8:38; Eph. 6:12; Col. 1:16; 2:15). Yet the same words are used elsewhere to describe human rulers (Luke 12:11; Acts 4:26). On other occasions, the distinction in Scripture is even less clear, and these words could describe either human or supernatural forces (Rom. 13:1; 1 Cor. 2:8; Titus 3:1).

The point of this is that the Bible recognizes the reality of both human authority and spiritual powers. It also depicts situations in which spiritual powers greatly influence human authority and the two operate together, sometimes without the human agency even being aware of the fact. Christians can be too ready and willing to accept the involvement of evil forces when it simply is not the case. Where a straightforward human explanation does exist, it is often far preferable to the suggestion of sinister spiritual influences being at work.

To many people it seems naïve and fanciful to suggest that issues such as apartheid and slavery could have their origins in the work of some unseen power. Both of these practices sought to achieve the degradation, humiliation, oppression, suffering, and practical enslavement of millions of people. Both had their roots in economic greed, false pride, fear, self-interest, and a distorted interpretation of Scripture. It is true that human beings carried out these dreadful practices, but it is difficult to ignore the possibility that they were motivated by unseen forces.

Once we acknowledge that powerful spiritual realities exist beyond ourselves, to see a diabolic strategy behind these awful deeds can scarcely be regarded as blind fantasy. After all, Scripture does warn us that "the god of this age has blinded ... minds" (2 Cor. 4:4).

Where do the powers operate? The Bible declares that they are all around us. Psalm 91:11, Matthew 4:6, and Hebrews 1:4–7 refer to angels of light, while Matthew 12:22–29, Luke 8:30–39, and Revelation 16:13–14 refer to those myriads of demons that form the nucleus of Satan's demon forces. These demons may attach themselves to specific territories or practices (Dan. 10:13; 12:1ff). They appear to be equally at home in "the Abyss," where we would most expect to find them, or in "the air," from which strategic vantage point they are ready and able to harass humankind (Luke 8:31; Eph. 2:2). These conquered satanic powers have yet to be tamed and domesticated. While they have no choice but to acknowledge the victory of Jesus over them, they still remain in a state of active rebellion against Him (Phil. 2:10). While their ultimate defeat has already been secured through the power of crucified love, they still attempt to exercise their pervasive influence throughout the earth.

10

THE FIGHT OF OUR LIVES

One fact about which most of us would probably wish to remain in a state of blissful ignorance is that the Holy Spirit does not normally go into battle alone. We would prefer that the fight did not actually involve us! The uncomfortable fact is that the Holy Spirit usually enters into combat with enemy powers by working in and through the people of God. In other words, we are quite likely to find ourselves on the front line!

Of course, when it comes to cosmic warfare, most of us are cowards at heart. We probably wish that we did not have to be involved, but the truth of the matter is that we were not recruited into the armies of the living God simply to engage in civilian pursuits. However unpleasant it may seem, the fact is that sometimes God calls His people to go to war, but at such moments, He arms them with superior power in the might and majesty of the Holy Spirit.

OPPOSING THE POWERS

In Ephesians 6:13, the apostle Paul instructs us to "put on the full armor of God" to prepare for battle, but none of the pieces of armor that God has provided is designed to protect our backs! They all operate on the assumption that we will only be moving forward. We are called upon to stand as the army of God, marching together under divine direction and sharing in the Spirit's victory over the powers.

We can be bold because our security lies in the one sure anti-dote against the powers of evil: the blood of Jesus Christ and the power of His Holy Spirit. In the Holy Spirit, true spiritual authority can be found and experienced. So while we might have preferred to remain a spiritual pacifist, at least we can know that we are on the winning side!

Jesus made a public example of the spiritual powers from the cross, unmasking them as enemies of the living God. Although the Roman system of justice and the Jewish religious structures were puppets, controlled by powers mightier than themselves, Jesus could still reign over them from a tree.

DEFEATING THE POWERS

From the cross, Jesus triumphed over the powers, but in His resurrection by the Holy Spirit, He actually penetrated and captured their territory. Jesus successfully invaded the realm of destruction and death and inflicted a resounding and total defeat upon the principalities and powers—on their home ground.

As Canon Michael Green has so acutely observed, "In Christ they were created (Col. 1:16) and in Christ they were defeated (Col. 2:15). Philippians 2:10 makes it quite plain that they must own His sway whether they like it or not. His Lordship, since the resurrection, has been beyond cavil among beings celestial, terrestrial and subterranean."[1]

It is true that spiritual warfare does have some similarities to physical conflicts. However, we need to be careful not to take the analogy too far, for while soldiers depend largely on physical strength and the necessary equipment for doing battle, the weapons of our spiritual war are those of compassion and self-giving love.

POWERS ON EARTH

One example of a spiritual battlefield lies in the realm of economics. Spiritual powers will always attempt to maintain an unfair distribution of resources so that the "haves" seize more and the "have-nots" receive less. By this means, they can create further injustice and cultivate resentment and bitterness among human beings. Their goals are quite simple: to create chaos and wreak havoc between people and nations by nurturing greed and the hunger for power. As long as Western societies make the availability of goods, economic prosperity, and the power that comes with it its ultimate goal, the spiritual powers will have won half of the battle.

But this is not just a problem that faces nations; it concerns individuals just as much. The Bible sternly denounces too great of a commitment to the accumulation of financial wealth and an unhealthy estimate of its importance. Jesus warned His disciples, "Be on your guard against all kinds of greed; a man's life does not consist in the abundance of his possessions" (Luke 12:15).

We may not feel comfortable in reading these words. Perhaps, we might think, they spring from a political bias. Or perhaps we are just envious of what God has given to others. We need to face the reality that a society that equates a "good standard of living" with how much money a person has is sadly out of line with what Jesus had to say on the matter. He pointed out that Christianity and materialism can never be comfortable bedfellows: "No one can serve two masters. . . . You cannot serve both God and Money" (Matt. 6:24).

In the Old Testament, God had already declared war on poverty. He announced that He was against a society where an unequal distribution of wealth was tolerated. It was a command rather than a prophecy when He instructed Israel, "There should be no poor among you" (Deut. 15:4). Jesus Himself lived in a state of relative poverty, and He had some pretty tough things to say to the rich. It was only when Zacchaeus offered generous compensation to those from whom he had embezzled and extorted money that Jesus could exclaim, "Today salvation has come to this house" (Luke 19:9).

While the Holy Spirit has certainly not necessarily been given to us to make us poor, He has come to sensitize us to the poverty of others and the need to actively support and care for all those less fortunate than ourselves. Ultimately it is not a matter of what we have received as a gift from God that is important, but it is the attitude we maintain toward our possessions and the generosity of spirit with which we are prepared to give them away.

There is actually no reason to feel guilty about what we have. It is only a gift from God, and it belongs to Him anyway. We should never be ashamed of what He has trusted us to steward for Him, nor should we despise it. But we should only hold lightly to what we have, recognizing that He can lay claim to whatever part that He wants at any moment that He chooses.

Rather than feeling guilty about what we have, we should acknowledge our responsibility for what we have been called to give away to meet the needs of our brothers and sisters. We should never feel guilty about what we have—only about our reluctance to give it away! What will always be more important than any feelings of guilt or remorse is the attitude that we maintain toward our possessions and the generosity of spirit we have when we receive divine instructions to give them away through the prompting of the Holy Spirit.

While we are to challenge and expose those injustices that are generated by spiritual powers, we also have another calling of God on our lives. Although we can do many things, there are many other areas that can be dealt with only by God Himself.

We are not only called on to confront injustice, but we are also called upon to pray—and pray strongly, vigorously, and continuously. Because the powers are evil, we must fervently pray to the One who is good in order that their strategies might be thwarted.

If we are to engage in effective spiritual warfare in prayer, we must realize that we cannot achieve it on our own. We must have the Holy Spirit's enabling if we are to pray effectively. Scripture places all of our spiritual abilities and resources in the simple context of our learning how to "pray in the Spirit on all occasions" (Eph. 6:18).

Our failure to recognize the existence of supernatural forces may be equaled only by our failure to recognize the power available to us in prayer. It is fair to ask whether major world events such as wars, man-made disasters, famines, civil unrest, or other catastrophes would have turned out differently—or been avoided altogether—if the church had risen to her God-given challenge of intercession against evil. If we would learn to accept the responsibility of praying constantly in the Holy Spirit, what might the God of heaven be able to accomplish on the earth? All of this may seem far removed from our usual and often casual spiritual experiences. It may not fit with the values or even the priorities that we currently adopt in our local church or fellowship. We may have been under the mistaken impression that the Holy Spirit was simply there to make our spiritual lives more fun or fulfilling. As we gaze in despair at our society and bemoan the condition into which it has fallen, we miss the real point: that this is the end result of enemy activity in our world, and that we have been called to do something about it.

It is only in our prayers, whether alone or with others, that we can combat the forces of evil. It is only as we pray that we can unlock the gates of heaven and see the living God release His grace and power upon us again. Human energies are completely inadequate for warfare against the powers. We have to realize that we will only see the triumph of Jesus reenacted among us as we pray in the power of the Holy Spirit.

We must not be content with murmuring a routine or ritual prayer on behalf of those in government. Paul insisted that we take spiritual warfare seriously. Jesus pointed out that a successful invasion of opposition territory is dependent upon our first being able to bind and immobilize the strong man (Matt. 12:24–29; Eph. 6:12)–which only happens through prayer. It would be naïve to think that we could ever see the rooting out of injustice and victory over the powers by any other means.

PRAYING AGAINST THE POWERS

To thwart successfully the attempted interference from evil powers, we must engage in the regular activity of committed intercession the way that God intended. The true measure of our concern for the poor and the powerless is seen not just in the level of our giving or personal involvement, but also in how we pray.

Whenever Satan uses his minions to frustrate the work of God, prayer is the immediate and appropriate defense. When the powers strike, we are called to strike back! The enemy often tries to interfere with the work of World Relief, and on those occasions when decisions are being made over the future direction of the work, we anticipate that spiritual warfare may be taking place.

At one strategic moment in the history of World Relief, we appointed a delightful African American couple to act as our full-time prayer coordinators. Although they both possessed quite a checkered past, this couple knew the Lord intimately and loved to pray. They appreciated only too well the nature and reality of spiritual warfare. For that reason, they anticipated that the enemy would want to interfere with our board's decisions. So for the duration of the board meetings, they stayed in the hall just outside the room where the board was conducting its deliberations and prayed. Except for short meal and restroom breaks, they stayed there for the entire thirty-six hours that the board met.

Imagine the surprise of the board members when they walked into the hall and saw this couple, with any staff members they could find, praying their hearts out for the board. Is it a coincidence that our board meetings are becoming more effective? No!

Time and again, before Jesus confronted the powers in His ministry here on earth, He always paused to pray. It is critical that we always seek to follow His example. The prayers of God's people will always prove to be the foundation on which our victory is built.

We are not called to run away from spiritual conflict or ignore the plight of the poverty-stricken. Instead, we are called upon to follow in the footsteps of the One who demonstrated over Satan by being born in a stable and dying unjustly on a cross. His life supremely showed that compassion toward others and dependence on His Father would cause the powers to shudder.

Whatever the powers may seek to throw at us, it is Jesus' example that we must follow. It is so that we may live our lives for Him that we are equipped by the Holy Spirit. It is in His service that we take our stand.

11

GIFTED BY GOD

When my children were young, I would often bring them presents when I came home from a trip. Although this was not an attempt to buy their love, it was successful in getting them to notice that I was back! However, sometimes they seemed to be more interested in the present I had brought than in the fact that I had returned. I didn't object too strongly because I knew that soon they would realize that a gift meant that the giver was not far away, and then they would turn their attention to Daddy. If they had ignored the gifts I had brought them and just left them unopened, I would probably have been offended!

The Holy Spirit is our gift from God, yet He in turn has many gifts to offer us. If we reject or ignore these gifts, we run the risk not only of insulting the Holy Spirit, but also the risk of unwittingly causing damage to ourselves and others. Most of these gifts are not just designed to benefit us, but they are also intended to help us help other people. When we use the gifts the Holy Spirit has given to us, we clearly show what it means to be part of the church of Jesus Christ. As Paul wrote to the Corinthians, "You are the body of Christ, and each one of you is a part of it" (1 Cor. 12:27).

Just as each part of our body has a role to play, so each one of us has a task in the body of Christ, His church. Just as a missing part in the body is instantly obvious and hampers every other part by its absence, so it is with the church.

Jesus always chose ordinary people through whom His Spirit could specifically express His gifts and love. The early church continued in the same pattern.

Because the church is the body of Jesus, it is not open to subdivision. This body cannot be divided into "gifted" and "non-gifted" sections. We all have a specific role to play in His eternal body, the church. Yet to live up to all that God has for us does not involve traveling a trouble-free road. He is with us, and He is for us, but that does not mean that our journey will be miraculously free of difficulty. So often He chooses to prepare us for the rest of our lives with Him through troubles and trials.

FOUR MAJOR PROBLEMS WE FACE

Specifically Jesus pioneered the way for us when He taught His disciples to triumph over four major problems that confronted them in their daily lives:

1. The problem of unknown potential (Luke 10:1—24)

By sending out seventy-two disciples, Jesus clearly demonstrated that learning to serve Him was not confined to just listening to His words. By going out together, these disciples destroyed the myth that the Lord will only use the spiritual elite, and they returned full of joy because of the way the Holy Spirit had used them.

Jesus did not send them on this journey of discovery alone. They traveled in twos, developing the potential in one another—and so should we. We must never attempt to live as a lone wolf for Jesus, but we must surrender to the divine influence of the Holy Spirit and permit Him to use our friends to develop our resources and potential.

2. The problem of wrong comparisons (Luke 21:1—4)

Many of us wonder if we have any use in God's kingdom. As we look at others whom God uses, we may see our gifts as totally insignificant. But Jesus showed that the poor widow who offered only a few coins gave a more meaningful offering than any of the leaders who contributed large sums of money, which they could easily afford.

3. The problem of being overly competitive (Luke 9:46–48)

Jesus forever settled all arguments as to who was the greatest among His disciples. We should not compete for gifts because it is the Holy Spirit who makes them available to us. If we are to stop devaluing ourselves and trust God's Spirit for all that we need for service, then we must be sure that we take no undue credit for His activities in our lives. What God chooses to do in the lives of His unlikely servants should bring credit only to the Lord.

4. The problem of fear (Luke 10:30–37)

The story of the Good Samaritan shows how easy it is to decline opportunities for service because of fear of the consequences. Many of us prefer a quiet life to a useful one. When the King of kings was crucified, He did not do so to gain a group of insipid and frightened disciples–they were that already. Instead, Jesus' purpose was always to die and save those who would, by the power of His Holy Spirit, possess lives so revolutionized that, as His people, they would boldly turn their world upside down.

FOR WHOM ARE THESE GIFTS GIVEN?

The answer to this question is simple: us!

An old story describes a Christian arriving at the gates of heaven. He was warmly greeted by the angel Gabriel, who offered a personally guided tour around the vastness of heaven. The first building they visited was an enormous aircraft hangar lined with narrow shelves. Each shelf was filled with neatly wrapped presents, all addressed to the new arrival.

"What's this?" asked the Christian.

"Oh, those," replied Gabriel, "they're all the gifts God had ready for you to use on the earth that you never bothered to claim!"

Perhaps this explains why Scripture is so plain and forceful on this point. The apostle Paul wrote to the church at Rome:

> Do not think of yourself more highly than you should.... We have many parts in the one body, and all these parts have different functions. In the same way, though we are many, we are one body in union with Christ, and we are all joined to each other as different parts of one body. So we are to use our different gifts in accordance with the grace that God has given us. If our gift is to speak God's message, we should do it according to the faith that we have; if it is to serve, we should serve; if it is to teach, we should teach; if it is to encourage others, we should do so. Whoever shares with others should do it generously; whoever has authority should work hard; whoever shows kindness to others should do it cheerfully.
>
> —ROMANS 12:3–8, GNT

There can surely be no more tragic obituary than "He ignored God's gifts and so failed to serve as he could have done."

WHAT ARE THESE GIFTS?

Several gifts are mentioned in the New Testament, although Christians do not agree on the exact number. Some have argued that God is raising up other gifts that are especially applicable to life in our world today, and so the following list is not meant to be exhaustive.

Some people believe that these gifts lost their value or even died out completely after the Scriptures were completed. But if this were true, it is certainly strange that the Scriptures themselves make no mention of that possibility. In any case, the twenty-seven gifts listed below clearly played a basic part in the life, ministry, and spiritual equipment of the local church during the first century of its existence.

1. The gift of discerning of spirits (1 Cor. 12:10; see also Luke 8:29)

2. The gift of the word of knowledge (1 Cor. 12:8; see also Luke 18:22)

3. The gift of the word of wisdom (1 Cor. 12:8; see also Luke 6:9)

4. The gift of tongues (Acts 19:6; 1 Cor. 12:10; 14:13–33)

5. The gift of prophecy (1 Cor. 12:10; 1 Thess. 5:20–21)

6. The gift of interpretation of tongues (1 Cor. 14:13)

7. The gifts of healing (1 Cor. 12:9; see also Acts 28:1–10)

8. The gift of faith (1 Cor. 12:9; see also Acts 3:6)

9. The gift of miracles (1 Cor. 12:10; see also Acts 6:8)

10. The gift of service (Rom. 12:7; see 2 Tim. 1:16–18)

11. The gift of teaching (Eph. 4:11–14)

12. The gift of motivation (Rom. 12:8; see also Acts 20:18–31)

13. The gift of giving (Rom. 12:8; see Acts 4:32–35)

14. The gift of leadership (Rom. 12:8; see Acts 13:12)

15. The gift of mercy (Rom. 12:8; see Luke 5:12–13)

16. The gift of apostle (Eph. 4:11)

17. The gift of hospitality (1 Pet. 4:9)

18. The gift of celibacy (1 Cor. 7:8)

19. The gift of administration (Acts 6:2–3)

20. The gift of exorcism (Acts 16:18)

21. The gift of evangelism (Eph. 4:11; 2 Tim. 4:5)

22. The gift of pastoral guidance (Eph. 4:11)

23. The gift of being a missionary (Eph. 3:7)

24. The gift of being willing to face martyrdom (1 Cor. 13:3)

25. The gift of helping (1 Cor. 12:28)

26. The gift of intercession (Rom. 8:26–27)

27. The gift of encouragement (Rom. 12:8; see also Heb. 10:24–25)

Each one of us is an individual, and God equips us with different gifts. Each gift is unique in itself although many of them complement each other. Most of the gifts can be used repeatedly, except, that is, for the gift of martyrdom! There is such a wide variety of gifts, and most of us are not limited to the possession of just one. In fact, if you can only identify one of these gifts in your life, then you probably have it in abundance!

WHAT ARE THE GIFTS FOR?

Because the church is Christ's body, it is a living organism in which Christ is the head and each one of us should be a vitally functioning part. There are three primary reasons God gives the gifts of the Holy Spirit:

1. To enable the members of the body of Christ to function properly

2. To enable the active participation of all of the members of the body of Christ

3. To represent the bounty of God and demonstrate, within the body of Christ, the beauty of God

As Simon the magician discovered in his confrontation with Simon Peter, a gift is simply that—a gift. We cannot buy it or earn it, nor should we use it for our own selfish purposes. It is to be used as God directs. Peter was both quick and direct in his response: "May your money perish with you, because you thought you could buy the gift of God with money! You have no part or

Gifted by God

share in this ministry, because your heart is not right before God"
(Acts 8:20–21).

WHAT DO WE KNOW ABOUT THE GIFTS?

Gifts are meant to be received, but they are also intended to be
used. God has entrusted them to us so that we may work for the
building of His kingdom, not using them for our own fulfillment
or entertainment. The privilege of these gifts involves the responsibility of our using them properly in the Lord's service.

Because each Christian has been given, and must be accountable
for, one or more gifts, our commitment to God can be seen in the
way we handle the gifts that have been entrusted to us. As Elizabeth
O'Connor has commented, "Commitment at the point of my gifts
means that I must give up being a straddler."[1]

Our responsibility extends to discovering, developing, and
using our gifts. Inspired by the Holy Spirit, the apostle Peter
clearly instructed his readers that "each one should use whatever
gift he has received to serve others, faithfully administering God's
grace in its forms" (1 Pet. 4:10).

Gifts are part of something called a "three-way giving." God gives
them to us, we offer them back to God, and by His Spirit He helps us
make them available to the whole church. Because the church is a
body, it is therefore a living organism; Christ is the head, and through
His Spirit, He makes each one of us vitally functioning parts!

The gifts of the Holy Spirit are not the same as our natural abilities. Everyone possesses some natural talent, but when a life is
committed to Jesus Christ, these talents can become gifts because
they become "saved" along with the rest of a personality. A "gift,"
however, is an ability given to an individual by God out of His love
and kindness, otherwise known as His "grace." The Greek word
charismata literally means "grace gifts," and within the strict
meaning of the word, it labels every Christian as a "charismatic"! A
ministry is actually the prolonged exercise of a gift. A gift is received
rather than achieved, and a ministry involves serving the body with
the gift that God has given.

81

Gifts are permanent because God never takes back what He has given. "God's gifts…are irrevocable" (Rom. 11:29). Our responsibility lies in the discovery, development, and use of God's gifts. In Romans 12:6, Paul encouraged the Roman Christians "to use [their] different gifts in accordance with the grace that God has given [them]" (Rom. 12:6, GNT). It is God's will and our welfare that are at stake!

Gifts will often overlap. An itinerant preacher could exhibit the gifts of missionary, evangelist, teacher, and prophet on the same weekend in a local church. Many will combine gifts such as motivation and administration in the same personality. In a special course at the Fuller School of World Mission, Carl Cronje said the following:

> Gifts must be distinguished from baseline responsibilities that all of us share equally; for example, all must pray, all must give, all must believe, but over and above the prayer that is demanded of all there is the gift of intercession; over and above the giving and believing required of all there is a gift of giving and a gift of faith. Gifts then are built on the baseline, they are the areas where we do far more than the minimum requirement. They are the areas where we find ourselves very comfortable in the Lord. They are the things that make us tick, the itch that only subsides when we scratch it with involvement and commitment. We are "in our element" when we are in our gifts![2]

Gifts are not to be graded. No one gift is more "spiritual" than another. As Paul wrote, "The eye cannot say to the hand, 'I don't need you!' On the contrary, those parts of the body that seem to be weaker are indispensable" (1 Cor. 12:21–22). Paul's whole point in 1 Corinthians 12 was that we should not regard the more seemingly "supernatural" gifts, such as speaking in tongues, to be superior to gifts that may seem more ordinary, like helping others and administration (1 Cor. 12:28). Nor should we be overly concerned about receiving false gifts. It is true that Satan can and does counterfeit God's gifts. But if our lives are totally surrendered to

Jesus, then He is the only one from whom we receive.

Jesus told His disciples, "If you then, though you are evil, know how to give good gifts to your children, how much more will your Father in heaven give the Holy Spirit to those who ask him!" (Luke 11:13).

WHAT MUST WE DO TO USE OUR GIFTS?

A friend of mine sometimes sings a song entitled "God Likes Me." These words always provoke a reaction. It seems impossible that, with all our failures and weaknesses, God should actually care about us, let alone entrust us with His gifts! Yet He does, and He even holds us accountable for how we have used them.

So, how do we receive the gifts of the Holy Spirit? In his excellent book *Your Spiritual Gifts Can Help Your Church Grow*, missiologist Peter Wagner suggests this line of discovery:

> An open mind and a teachable spirit are essentials. If we feel we know it all or are too proud to be corrected, we will not function optimally. Some practical suggestions in this regard are:
>
> 1. Explore all the possibilities by learning the biblical facts about gifts.
>
> 2. Experiment with as many as you can. Try to find your aptitude this way. This can be done sincerely. Don't be afraid to fail. It is also important to know what gifts we don't have.
>
> 3. Examine your feelings. Your interests and your aptitudes when merging will give the greatest success. You will feel comfortable in your gift.
>
> 4. Evaluate your effectiveness. Don't be too proud to admit where you have not had success. Also don't be so (falsely) "humble" as to deny where God is using you.
>
> 5. Expect confirmation from your brothers and sisters. We are often the last to see things about ourselves that

are obvious to others at a glance. This is true submission—i.e. teamwork, knowing where our boundaries of effectiveness are by mutual consultation.

6. Exert caution with regard to the particular peril of your gift. For most privileges there is a peril and this is especially true of God's gifts.[3]

The gifts and talents that the Holy Spirit would bring to our lives are not designed to be used in isolation. We are to complement other Christians whose gifts will be different from our own.

To that end, we need to be careful to recognize those gifts that God has given to us—and those that He has not. As J. B. Phillips has paraphrased Romans 12:3: "Try to have a sane estimate of your capabilities" (PHILLIPS). We should be prepared to experiment and discover from the positive response (or otherwise) of other Christians whether a particular gift is really from God or the product of our own fertile imagination!

I was talking to a young evangelist once, when he blurted out, "I get so scared. I feel so ill before preaching; I just don't know if evangelism is my gift or not!" Now, if God has really given us a gift or talent, results will inevitably follow, so I asked him what response came from his preaching. "Oh, nearly always people are converted, often several come to real repentance," he replied. I simply encouraged him to keep feeling scared! That was a small price to pay for the privilege of using God's gift.

Another incorrect idea that seems to be popular in evangelical Christianity is that God *only* uses us in those areas in which we feel uncomfortable! That is by no means the case. God often uses us in our areas of strength. He can also bring surprising new areas of giftings to us—after all, He made us, and He knows both who we are and what we need. It is as we place ourselves unreservedly in God's hands that He will gift us for His service. Our duty is not to do God's work for Him or to ask Him to bless our plans, schemes, or inclinations. Instead, it is to respond to God's initiatives in our lives by obedience to the gifts that He places within us.

As Peter Wagner put it:

> Every spiritual gift we have is a resource which we must
> use and for which we will be held accountable at the judg-
> ment. Some will have one, some two and some five. The
> quantity, to begin with, does not matter. Stewards are
> responsible only for what the master has chosen to give
> them but the resource that we do have must be used to
> accomplish the master's purpose.[4]

As we open ourselves up, we cease trying to insist that everyone
has the same gifts we do; and we are free to let each one be himself. Some of our gifts may be more obvious than others, and we
may never cease discovering the gifts that God will add to all of
our lives. At this level, we demonstrate what it means to truly love
and serve Jesus, not in our own strength but in the power and
authority that God gives.

Finally, we must remember one all-important truth: Jesus, as
God's greatest Gift, did not come to earth as some vague, ethereal
force. The miracle of the Incarnation lies in the fact that He came
as a real person. We must always remember to give God not just
the use of our talents—but also our entire selves.

GIFTS THAT SOMETIMES CAUSE A PROBLEM!

The Christian church traces its origins back to the Day of Pentecost, where it had its true start (Acts 2:1–13). In Acts 11:15, Peter commented that the Holy Spirit came upon the Gentiles as He had come on them at the beginning. Right away the church recognized the divinity of the Holy Spirit. Immediately His identity and His general ministry were accepted without controversy. In many of the writings of the early church, there is little written specifically about the Holy Spirit because He is spoken about in the context of the Trinity rather than as a specific subject in His own right.

One significant exception to this general rule was the second-century theologian Irenaus. He offered his own unequivocal testimony to the Holy Spirit's importance when he pointed out that in "receiving the Holy Spirit, we walk in newness of life, in obedience to God. Without the Spirit of God, we cannot be saved."[1]

Many of the gifts of the Holy Spirit have been joyfully accepted by God's people throughout the centuries to the present day. The church has recognized these gifts in every age. But other gifts have proved to be more controversial. Some of the "supernatural" gifts outlined in 1 Corinthians 12:8–10 were almost totally ignored for centuries. Many people run from things they cannot understand. But in doing so, they reflect the spirit of the age rather than the Holy Spirit. Human beings prefer to pattern things so that we can show how, neatly packaged, they fit into our understanding. God, on the other hand, longs to see us break away from all our presuppositions, pride, and prejudices. His purposes cannot be shackled to our understanding of how they should be performed!

If God is to be God, then He must reign. It is easy to sing songs such as "Our God Reigns," but then we try to conform Him to the way we prefer to operate. Our reluctance to see the Lord break through our established norms says more of our lack of flexibility and openness to His will and purpose than anything else.

Two hundred years ago, John Wesley wrote these words:

> It does not appear that these extraordinary gifts of the Holy Ghost were common in the church for more than two or three centuries. We seldom hear of them after that fatal period when the Emperor Constantine called himself a Christian.... From this time they almost totally ceased; very few instances of the kind were found. The cause of this was not... "because there was no more occasion for them."... The real cause was, "the love of many," almost of all Christians, so-called, was "waxed cold."...This was the real cause why the extraordinary gifts of the Holy Ghost were no longer to be found in the Christian Church.[2]

These gifts can be placed in three groupings:

1. Gifts of revelation (the power to know): discerning of spirits, word of knowledge, and word of wisdom

2. Gifts of activity (the power to do): gifts of healing, working of miracles, and gift of faith

3. Gifts for communication (the power to say): gift of tongues, gift of interpretation, and gift of prophecy

OBJECTION!

There are those who would stop at this point to protest. Three objections have been given to the use of these gifts today.

1. "We don't need these gifts."

This argument states that, throughout history, God has worked in different ways at different times; supernatural gifts were necessary in the early days, but now, with the completion of the Bible and the establishment of the church, we have no further need for a demonstration of the power of God.

There is something to be said for this line of argument, for the Spirit has been more active in some periods than in others. However, it possesses two fatal flaws.

First, it seems to be an argument based primarily on experience and then rationalized by Scripture, starting with a lack of supernatural "evidence" and moving to create an explanation. It is always safer to move from Scripture first, and then to experience. Anything other than this is unreliable because instead of allowing Scripture to mold our experience, we tend to allow our defective experience to shape our interpretation.

Second, while claiming to elevate the authority of Scripture, it fails to do justice to the truth of Scripture. There is nothing in Scripture that suggests these gifts are not for the people of Christ in every age. An honest look at Scripture leads us to anticipate everything that is a part of our birthright.

2. "These gifts focus our attention on the wrong person."

The Holy Spirit does not seek to bring attention to Himself because His function is to bear witness to Jesus. This argument states that there is a danger in the way that these extraordinary gifts can focus undue attention on either the Holy Spirit, the gift itself, or the person exercising the gift.

Many people have been carried away with their own importance in the exercise of a gift, and errors have been made—but this also happened in the early church. Paul's reminders to the Corinthian Christians were designed to correct exactly that kind of mistake. But the abuse did not mean that the practice should be stopped.

One safeguard could be put into place to prevent these problems from occurring. These gifts should be practiced in the context of a local church or fellowship with the accompanying structured authority.

3. "The gifts of the Spirit are not as important as the fruit."

Two Christians were talking together, and one said to the other, "Well, you can have the gifts. I'll take the fruit." My response to that would be to suggest that I would rather not choose—I want to have all that God has to offer! Quite honestly, I need all the help I can get!

We need to recognize and value both the fruit and the gifts; both are produced by the Holy Spirit in the life of the believer, but each should be carefully evaluated alongside the teaching of Scripture. We will never begin to understand the significance of either the fruit or the gifts until we view them in the proper context of the Person and work of the Holy Spirit. It is who the Holy Spirit is that determines what He does.

The simple fact is that the gifts of the Holy Spirit represent various ways in which the power of God works in and through the life of the believer. The fruit of the Holy Spirit is the character and nature of Jesus Christ being shown in the life of the believer. Jesus did not only say to the sick who came to Him, "I love you," but He also said, "Be healed!"

Surely one of the saddest things to experience is to love someone and yet be incapable of helping them. We should always accept everything that God offers, even if it creates theological problems for us!

First Corinthians 12 and 14, containing Paul's teaching on gifts, are like a sandwich, with his teaching on love in the middle. Sometimes people say that love is the greatest of the gifts, but this is not what Paul was saying. If we read 1 Corinthians 12:31 and then go on to 14:1, it says: "But eagerly desire the greater gifts. And now I will show you the most excellent way.... Follow the way of love and eagerly desire spiritual gifts, especially the gift of prophecy." Paul is pleading for the exercise of all of the gifts *in love*, the working together of the fruit and the gifts of the Spirit.

Ignoring the gifts at one level is foolish; at another it is just plain impolite. If we choose to ignore these gifts, we are running risks in two major areas. First, by removing the supernatural ingredient from Christianity, we give an open invitation to Satan to fascinate society by his own subtle but completely inferior tricks. And second, when we ignore the gifts, we can reduce Christianity to the status of an alternative philosophy. The emphasis on miracles in Jesus' personal ministry should encourage us to see our faith in the context of the supernatural activity of the living God among men and women.

However, as we may be unfamiliar with these gifts and because they have caused both disagreement and division due to the dangers associated with their abuse, we must look in a little more detail at what the Bible has to say about them.

THE POWER TO KNOW

1. Discerning of spirits

The discerning of spirits is different from a person's own natural judgment. It is the mind of Christ being revealed through a believer. This is a necessary defense, particularly where the gifts are concerned. We need to differentiate between what comes from God, what comes from the enemy, and what comes from ourselves. Jesus warned His disciples not to allow themselves to be deceived: "Watch out that no one deceives you" (Matt 24:4). The warning was a necessary one. Peter could know in an instant who Jesus really was through revelation that could only have come from the Father, but in the next moment Jesus had to rebuke him. "'Get behind me, Satan,' he said. 'You do not have in mind the things of God, but the things of men'" (Mark 8:33).

2. Word of knowledge

This is the supernatural revelation by God of information that was not learned by the effort of our natural minds. Jesus demonstrated this gift when He saw the real need in the life of the

Samaritan woman. "'Come, see a man who told me everything I ever did,'" she said (John 4:29). This gift enabled Peter to expose the corruption in Ananias and Sapphira (Acts 5:1–11). Christian counselors sometimes experience that quiet moment when God reveals to their heart the real problem beneath the surface issues that are dominating the conversation. What to do with that information poses a different problem, and for that, God has another answer.

3. Word of wisdom

The word of wisdom constitutes supernatural revelation as to what action needs to be taken in a given situation, often after the word of knowledge has first been given to expose the exact nature of the problem.

We need to be careful at this point. Sometimes we try to give God a helping hand, but even if it is for the best possible reasons, what we then say ceases to be His message and becomes ours. We need the help of other Christians to confirm that what is said and done has truly come from God alone.

A few years ago, while in a prayer meeting, I spoke out a message that I felt to be from God. I suppose that I had the confidence to do so because I knew that there were friends there who would test the message. Imagine my dismay, on looking up for confirmation, to see one friend shaking his head. Crestfallen, I crept over to him. "What was wrong?" I asked.

"The first two sentences were from God," he replied. "The rest was your own excellent, but human, assistance."

That check meant two things. I would not blunder on aimlessly, failing to realize my mistake, and because I had the loving support of those who could discern error, I would not lose confidence. God does not want a people constantly holding back, nor does He want a people who launch out alone. Each one of us needs the correction of discerning friends.

Usually more than one person will have the same revelation if it is of God. As we progress in the life of the Spirit, our ability to hear the Lord will develop. But don't be surprised in the meantime if He gives you a helpful nudge!

THE POWER TO DO

1. Gifts of healing

Ninety percent of the recorded ministry of Jesus on earth was devoted to healing the sick. His first instruction to His disciples when He sent them out was to "heal the sick" (Matt. 10:8). After His death and resurrection, Jesus Himself performed no further healings. Healing from then on was part of His commission to His disciples.

Immediately after the Day of Pentecost, the disciples began to heal the sick, raise the dead, and cast out demons. In so doing, they were only fulfilling the words of Jesus: "I tell you the truth, anyone who has faith in me will do what I have been doing" (John 14:12).

2. Working of miracles

While "gifts of healing" refer to God's curing physical conditions in the human body, other events come under the heading of "miracles." Miraculous signs were a large part of God's provision for the children of Israel, and they were a constant feature in the life of Jesus and in the experience of the early church. Prison escapes were arranged (Acts 5:17–25; 12:1–17; 16:25–40). Paul survived the bite of a deadly snake with no side effects (Acts 28:3–6). And in recent years, miraculous events have been documented all over the world.

The purpose of a miracle is to meet a human need and, in line with the continuing ministry of the Holy Spirit, to bring glory to Jesus. If a miracle fulfills any other purpose, be careful; Satan can produce all kinds of demonic counterfeit miracles, but they will never glorify Jesus!

3. The gift of faith

From the moment we are born again, faith begins to operate. When we learn to trust Jesus, we become open to the faith that the Holy Spirit produces as a fruit in our lives. However, it can also operate as a special gift in our lives, just as Daniel experienced it in

92

the den of lions and as Elijah waited in full confidence for God's dramatic intervention on Mount Carmel (Dan. 6:17–28; 1 Kings 18:21; James 5:17–18).

The "power to do" comes from the Holy Spirit and always operates in line with Scripture. God's power does not diminish with time. His Spirit is not running down in power like a battery; He is still active today.

We do need, however, to distinguish between faith and foolishness. The Holy Spirit will not just do whatever we demand. He brings glory to Jesus and only acts in accordance with the will of the Father. As God, He does not live in obedience to us. If we would see God at work among us, we must not blunder into situations that angels would leave well alone! Nor should we be guilty of raising people's expectation of a healing or miracle, only to see their hopes dashed to the ground. It is only as we ask God to lead us into His way, and confirm it with our brothers and sisters, that we can move out in confidence. What God has told us to do, that He will honor.

THE POWER TO SAY

1. The gift of tongues
The gift of tongues is the ability to praise God in an unknown language. This language may originate on earth or in heaven. We shall say more about the place of this gift in worship in a later chapter.

2. The gift of interpretation
The gift of interpretation is the ability to understand what is being said when someone speaks in tongues. Without it, tongues would remain incomprehensible.

3. The gift of prophecy
The gift of prophecy brings a message from God, often spontaneously, that is relevant to a particular situation. Prophecy is singled out by the apostle Paul as a gift that we should actively

seek: "Therefore, my brothers, be eager to prophesy" (1 Cor. 14:39). It is not a private gift but one that should always be evaluated by other believers present. Although prophecy can be relevant for unbelievers, its primary function is to provide "help, encouragement, and comfort" for Christians (1 Cor. 14:3, GNT).

The power to speak God's Word should produce powerful and direct results. Hearing God speak through ordinary people in this way should lead unbelievers to conclude, "God is really among you!" (v. 25). This power may operate through preaching or prayer. Prophetic praying or preaching can be a truly effective vehicle in God's hands when we surrender our words to His control.

These supernatural gifts and the exercise of them should be labeled, "Handle With Care!" They must be carefully developed under the authority of a local church or fellowship. But we must not let the dangers inherent in their operation prevent us from allowing God to give us these gifts if He wishes. As Bishop Gavin Reid concluded in the Church of England newspaper some years ago:

> The plain fact of the matter is that even the best evangelical religion bears little resemblance to the experience of the Apostles. We have conditioned ourselves not to notice this.... Is there any good reason why the charismatic element in the New Testament should not continue throughout history? Should we play down evidences of a supernatural God in case they might disturb the weaker brother? Surely if God is working, we should shout it from the housetops. And if our shouting upsets the apple cart—amen to that![3]

It is as we open ourselves up to the Lord that He can give us His gifts and teach us to use them. We must do our part to be sure that the glory never goes to the gift or to the recipient of the gift, but to the One who is Himself the Giver of every good and perfect gift. Our responsibility is to use these gifts to build up one another and extend the ministry of the kingdom of God.

For this reason, the apostle Peter urged:

Gifts That Sometimes Cause a Problem!

Each one should use whatever gift he has received to serve others, faithfully administering God's grace in its various forms. If anyone speaks, he should do it as one speaking the very words of God. If anyone serves, he should do it with the strength God provides, so that in all things God may be praised through Jesus Christ. To him be the glory and the power for ever and ever. Amen.

—1 PETER 4:10–11

13

POWER TO BE WITNESSES

Some years ago, an American airliner, crammed full of passengers, crashed into the muddy and icy waters of the Potomac River, just a few miles from where I live today. Amid all of the frantic rescue attempts, a helicopter arrived on the scene, trailing a rope with a lifebelt attached. Sighting an elderly man desperately clinging to some floating wreckage, the crew lowered the rope, but the man rejected it, and instead of using the lifebelt himself, he chose to attach it to someone else.

Feverishly the men in the helicopter pulled up the survivor and let down the line to the drowning man. Yet again, he saw another person needing help and gave him the lifebelt. A third time the lifebelt was lowered—but by then the elderly man was gone, leaving only the wreckage floating on the surface.

Two thousand years ago, the Son of God voluntarily relinquished His own life in order to save others. Through His death, He offered Paradise to a dying thief, forgiveness to His failed disciple, Peter, and His Spirit to His friends.

That last action was to be crucially important. It provides us with the only real explanation for how 120 assorted men and women, distinguished only by an absence of theological qualifications, would soon turn their whole world upside down. These ordinary folk, who gathered together some two thousand years ago around a shared belief that a dead carpenter was actually alive, began a movement that today can claim an active worldwide membership in excess of one billion people.[1]

No human agency could have achieved this. It lay beyond the realm of natural explanation, but that is exactly what happened. The initial dramatic growth of the church was not achieved by military conquest or any other type of enforcement, but through a convicting Spirit sent from heaven to lead people toward a genuine, life-changing, personal conversion.

THE HOLY SPIRIT IN EVANGELISM

The lives of ordinary people are not permanently transformed by human initiative or man-made ingenuity, but only by the power of the Holy Spirit. Divine intervention is absolutely necessary for the salvation of men and women, and without the gift of the Holy Spirit, the incredible spread of the gospel in the early days of the church could never have happened. When the Holy Spirit came to tired, frustrated, and frightened men hiding behind locked doors, He transformed them into those powerful witnesses who, in a few short years, would have carried the good news of Jesus Christ throughout the then known world. This was a miracle!

Jesus refused to permit His disciples to set foot outside of Jerusalem until they had first received His Spirit, who would provide all the resources that they would need to fulfill the great task that He had entrusted into their hands. He instructed them to be "my witnesses in Jerusalem, in all of Judea and Samaria, and to the ends of the earth" (Acts 1:8). But before that would take place, they had to wait patiently for His power. This lesson was an important one because the work of God cannot, and must not, be attempted only in the strength of man.

As one contemporary prophet, A. W. Tozer, has reminded us:

> The popular notion that the first obligation of the church is to spread the gospel to the uttermost parts of the earth is false. Her first obligation is to be spiritually worthy to spread it. Our Lord said, "Go ye," but He also said, "Tarry ye," and the tarrying had to come before the going. Had the

disciples gone forth as missionaries before the day of Pentecost, it would have been an overwhelming spiritual disaster, for they could have done no more than make converts after their own likeness.[2]

WAITING FOR GOD

So just what is the spiritual condition of America today?

I have heard many people tell me how desperately weak and spiritually poor they feel that the United States is now, especially in comparison to the past. Many seem to be actively predicting that disaster is lurking just around the corner. There are those who talk of "time running out." Some even seem to fear that there is little hope left!

Yet if we were to ask the opinion of those outside of the U.S., a very different picture would emerge. Far from viewing the States as a godless society, much of the world envies the U.S. for her spirituality.

My homeland of Britain is not as spiritual of a nation. Thirty-five percent of Britain's churches have fewer than twenty-five members. Indeed, less than 10 percent of the churches there have two hundred members or more. Many other countries, especially in Western Europe, have large numbers of very small churches, but what is strange is that nearly 90 percent of their younger generations have never even heard of who Jesus is. Yet we still call these countries "spiritual" or even "Christian."[3]

In both America and Europe, the spread of pornography, unrestricted abortion, and occult practices has reached unprecedented peaks. Against this trend, just about every new concept in evangelism has been tried; each new "gimmick," idea, program, and resource has been used—and found to be wanting. Jesus has called us to be His witnesses, but at least in spiritual terms, the Western world just seems to be heading downhill.

Meanwhile the rest of the world is seeing the greatest move of God that has been experienced in the history of the church. One Korean congregation now tops eight hundred thousand members—and is still growing. During the twentieth century alone, Latin

America witnessed a rise from fifty thousand believers in 1900 to estimated figures of one hundred million Christians by now![4] That kind of phenomenal growth was also paralleled in large parts of Africa. But still Western Europe seems obsessed with a passion for "spirituality" in its vaguest form, and the concern for a Christian life is now sadly missing. Furthermore, North America seems to be traveling rapidly in the same direction.

Could it be that the living God is waiting for timid, frightened Christians hiding away in cozy evangelical ghettoes to begin to call on Him for the kind of revival that is currently being seen in the rest of the world? The fantastic growth of prayer groups and cells in the last decade is a wonderful indication of all that God could still do among us. More than three hundred years ago, the great Puritan scholar Matthew Henry said, "When God intends great mercy for His people, the first thing He does is to set them a-praying."[5]

When God attempts a mighty move within a nation, He does not reserve His resources for only the "spiritual elite." The Lord longs to take hold of each one of us and make us into His messengers to our dying land. "Yes, even on my servants, both men and women, I will pour out my Spirit in those days, *and they will proclaim my message*" (Acts 2:18, GNT, emphasis added).

It is not for us to seize the rope and only rescue ourselves. Our task is to hand the rope on to those suffering around us. It is the Holy Spirit who provides the rope. He gives us the words to say and the authority with which to deliver them. He takes insignificant, ordinary people and transforms them into powerful witnesses for Jesus Christ—with their lives as well as with words that speak the truth. It is our job to get on with the task that we have been given.

WHAT ARE WE TO SAY?

Jesus promised that His followers would never be left without the words to speak. He said:

> When you are brought before synagogues, rulers and authorities, do not worry about how you will defend

yourselves or what you will say, for the Holy Spirit will
teach you at that time what you should say.

—LUKE 12:11–12

Despite that reassurance from the Lord Himself, many of us are
reluctant to allow God the opportunity to speak through us. We
doubt our ability, and we question our intelligence or understanding. Moses had similar fears, but God's reply was blunt.
"Moses said to the LORD, 'O Lord, I have never been eloquent.... I
am slow of speech and tongue.' The LORD said to him, 'Who gave
man his mouth?'" (Exod. 4:10–11).

There are many people who have made the opposite response—
their new life's ambition is to talk to someone about Jesus every
day. They may not feel gifted, or even able, but they trust the Holy
Spirit to use them and honor their offer of a mouth for Him to fill.

One Anglican bishop occasionally becomes bored on a train
journey. Rather than turning to a magazine or a book to pass the
time, he instead walks into a compartment and asks, "Can anyone
tell me who Jesus Christ really is?" As people look up, startled and
embarrassed, trying to hide behind newspapers, he sits down to
answer his question for them!

Not all of us would be able to repeat this performance! I know
that I so often fail to share my faith. Yet the Holy Spirit comes into
our lives to enable us to become bolder in our faith, not just for
our own blessing and edification. He comes to empower us to
meet the needs of others. He is, first and foremost, a missionary
Spirit who helps us to fulfill the work and will of God by bringing
others to Jesus.

In order to achieve this goal, the Holy Spirit produced three dis-
tinct characteristics in the lives of the early believers. He was at work
in them to:

- Promote compassionate actions (Acts 6:1–3).
- Demonstrate spiritual power (Acts 6:8).
- Generate bold proclamation (Acts 7:52).

Power to Be Witnesses

The Holy Spirit became the "energizer" of the early church as it communicated the love of Jesus Christ, first to Jerusalem, and then to the ends of the known world. He provided the spontaneous direction as to where and when the good news should be shared, and He generated the believers' desire to share their faith through public preaching, demonstrative lifestyles, and personal witness. He took advantage of the everyday situations in the lives of ordinary Christians to promote further opportunities for effective witnessing. In that way, their outreach was not a learned method or process, but it was something that came naturally. The believers discovered that they couldn't keep from "gossiping the gospel" and sharing the truth they had found in the power of the Holy Spirit (1 Pet. 1:12).

When faced with hostility, opposition, and even persecution, they were still compelled to proclaim the truth of Jesus Christ. One great example is the apostle Paul. Despite many hazards to his personal health and safety, he never stopped declaring the good news of Jesus Christ to all who would listen. His motivation was the loving compulsion of the Holy Spirit (Rom. 5:5; 1 Cor. 9:16; 2 Cor. 5:14).

This spontaneous overflow of love did not just happen in Paul's life; it infected everyone in the early church. No wonder their growth was so dramatic! The much-loved American sociologist and preacher Tony Campolo never tires of reminding his hearers, "The Book of Acts, baby, the Book of Acts!" because that is the book that tells of the amazing exploits of the Holy Spirit. When we consider the way the Holy Spirit still wants to move through the people of God today, nothing much has changed in the past two thousand years!

One story from the nineteenth century illustrates the point. The great American evangelist D. L. Moody made a promise to God shortly after his conversion that twenty-four hours would never pass without his sharing Jesus with someone else. One night he realized he had not kept his word. He hurried out of bed, fearing he wouldn't find anyone to whom he could witness, but there was a man standing under a lamppost. He walked over and asked this perfect stranger, "Are you a Christian?" The man was embarrassed, antagonistic, and extremely offended, and he had no problem saying so!

Moody was crestfallen. What a mistake! Maybe he should have been less blindly enthusiastic.

Many of us would never have done such a thing, but God honors the efforts of those who do, those who see the opportunity and have the character to take advantage of it.

Weeks passed by. One night Moody was in bed when he heard a tremendous pounding at his front door. He jumped out of bed and rushed to the door. He thought that perhaps his house was on fire and someone was trying to break down the door. Outside stood the man Moody had witnessed to under the lamppost. He said, "Mr. Moody, I have not had a good night's sleep since that night you spoke to me, and I have come here at this unearthly hour of the night to find out how to be saved." Moody led the man to Jesus. Soon afterward the man died, but because of Moody's spiritual aggression, he will spend eternity with Jesus Christ![6]

WHAT ARE WE TO KNOW?

Only the Holy Spirit can take us through the doubts of our contemporary world and move us to the certainty of what God has for us in Jesus. "He is the Spirit, who reveals the truth about God" (John 14:17, GNT).

The Holy Spirit is the only One who fully knows all that Jesus really wants to say to us. As Paul affirmed, "This is what we speak, not in words taught us by human wisdom but in words taught by the Spirit, expressing spiritual truths in spiritual words" (1 Cor. 2:13). Not only does the Holy Spirit equip us as God's servants to teach, but He also enables us to learn.

The Spirit has been given to lead us into all truth. And this truth is to be lived out, not just believed. We must never sacrifice truth on the altar of our own limited spiritual experience, nor should we be satisfied with the *knowledge* of the truth at the expense of *experiencing* the truth.

How we handle the truth that God gives us is of vital importance. If we have come to a greater degree of God's truth than our neighbor has, it is not an occasion for self-satisfaction or self-congratulation. That would be little more than a demonstration of human pride in operation.

Truth and character should always live in harmony together. For example, if we meet someone in whose life the Holy Spirit is obviously at work, we should be careful not to immediately denounce him on the grounds of doctrinal error because he believes differently than us. Rather we should rejoice wholeheartedly at the way God is speaking to that person, but without compromising truth. We must be ready for the opportunity to point out graciously the differences in our convictions.

It is often a stunning rebuke when we realize that those who have less of an understanding of the Scriptures actually excel us in terms of love, worship, and service. If that is the case, should we reject the truth that we have come to accept? By no means! Jesus Himself was "full of grace *and* truth" (John 1:14, emphasis added). Both are important—we cannot emphasize one and neglect the other. Failure to demonstrate grace with truth can be as damaging as choosing to sacrifice truth in order to be more acceptable to others. We should hold tenaciously to the truth, but we should also learn to disagree with others without being disagreeable ourselves. As I have come to say, "We need to learn what it means to *walk* our *talk*."

The Holy Spirit is not content with only feeding our minds. He wants to change the way we feel as well as the way we think. Believers in the United States have so much information about spiritual matters in the form of conferences, books, tapes, and workshops. We have boundless resources to help us advance in the Christian life, more than believers in any other country in the world. But so often we fail to learn because we are bogged down with doubts, guilt, and fear. Our constant cry is, "How can I be sure?" As Martin Luther would have crisply informed us, "The art of doubting is easy, for it is an ability that is born in us."[7]

It is the Holy Spirit who comes with a divine answer: "I pray that out of his [God] glorious riches he may strengthen you with power through his Spirit in your inner being" (Eph. 3:16). Not content with just supplying the answers, the Holy Spirit also brings us the faith to believe them. The Holy Spirit is the supreme evangelist. He has come to guide people toward the truth, because He is Himself the Spirit of truth (John 14:17; 16:3; 1 John 4:6). It is by the Spirit that people are convicted of sin. He is the author of new life and brings us into the reality of being born into a new life in Jesus (John 3:6–8; 6:63; 16:7–8; 2 Cor. 3:6; 1 Pet. 3:18). He gives the assurance that our salvation has been accomplished through crucified love and that it is secure (Rom. 8:16; Gal. 4:6; 1 John 3:2; 4:13; 5:6).

WHAT ARE WE TO DO?

God can speak volumes through lives that are touched by the beauty of the Holy Spirit. Witnessing for Jesus is often more a matter of lifestyle than anything else. Our words should never have to be more than an explanation of our lives. Our modern culture seems to demand to "view the evidence" before they "believe the words." This can be seen in the state of Missouri's nickname—the "Show Me State."

It is through the power and intervention of the Holy Spirit that we begin to resemble Jesus. In our own strength, we cannot change ourselves into signposts that point away from ourselves and draw others to Christ. Only the Holy Spirit can release us from all that we have been and begin to mold us into a different likeness. "Where the Spirit of the Lord is, there is freedom. And we, who with unveiled faces all reflect the Lord's glory, are being transformed into his likeness with ever-increasing glory, which comes from the Lord, who is the spirit" (2 Cor. 3:17–18).

The search for this different kind of lifestyle has gone on throughout the centuries. Nicodemus came to Jesus for one reason. Although he was the equivalent of a theology professor at the University of Jerusalem, he recognized that Jesus possessed something that he did not have—the power to live life as God intended. Jesus' response to him was very significant: "That which is born of the flesh is flesh, and that which is born of the Spirit is spirit" (John 3:6, NKJV).

In other words, Jesus was saying that without the Spirit, we will never make it.

Only through the presence of the Spirit can we begin to love Jesus in such a way as to fulfill the words of Bernard of Clairvaux: "What a man loves he will grow to look like."

The Spirit wants to place the love and compassion of Jesus within our lives. He wants to make us into people who will pour out our hearts day after day for our non-Christian neighbors and friends; who will weep for them; who will become involved in the needs and work of the community to build bridges for Jesus; who will always have an ear to listen and a heart to love those who need help. Because of the empowering of the Holy Spirit, a people will emerge from the shadows of a fearful Christian witness into a free, bold expression of the life of Jesus within them. Some will focus on words, some on acts of mercy, some on prayer, and some on lifestyle. But through each one, the Holy Spirit will work out His divine purposes.

HOW TO MAKE A DIFFERENCE

Jesus has commissioned all of His disciples to be His witnesses: "All authority in heaven and on earth has been given to me. Therefore go and make disciples of all nations" (Matt. 28:18–19). And Jesus had the authority to both send and equip them for this task.

As disciples of Christ today, we must recognize our inability to be effective witnesses apart from His strength. Without the Holy Spirit, we can only experience the following:

- A reluctance to share our faith
- A failure to pray
- A lack of love and compassion for those around us
- Isolation from our community

- Cowardice when we should have been a witness for Christ

And yet, despite our failures, God provides us with His Spirit. When we confess our inadequacy to the Father, when we stop trying to serve God in our own human abilities, we can then plug in to divine resources and receive the power we need to be effective witnesses for Christ. Our words can be replaced by the Holy Spirit's words, our life by His life, our compassion by His compassion, and our prayer life by His prayer life. All of this can take place through the intervention of the Spirit of God Himself.

E. Stanley Jones, the great missionary pioneer, used to say that evangelism was simply one beggar telling another where to find bread. In other words, we ourselves possess only a few resources, but as we allow the Holy Spirit to control our lives, He gives us the message and provides the resources and encouragement for its delivery. Such a life might not be easy, but it is fruitful.

Perhaps, with the Spirit's help, we might ourselves echo the famous words of missionary pioneer C. T. Studd:

> Let us not glide through this world and then slip quietly into heaven, without having blown the trumpet loud and long for our Redeemer, Jesus Christ. Let us see to it that the devil will hold a thanksgiving service in hell when he gets the news of our departure from the field of battle.[8]

14

NOT JUST FOR ME!

Sometimes we are so focused on the fact that the Holy Spirit has made His home in our individual lives that we forget He has also come to make us a part of a whole new family. We forget that this same Holy Spirit was the midwife who birthed the church of Jesus Christ. Not only does the Spirit bring the joys of *personal* salvation to our lives, but He also introduces us into a new *community*—in fact, a whole new type of society!

The Holy Spirit is the guarantee that we will belong to this family forever. There will come a point in history when the Lord Jesus will return to take His bride, the church. One day we will reign together with King Jesus, but until that time arrives, we are to act as His hands and feet on the earth.

For this reason, the Holy Spirit has been assigned as our Helper in this life. Because of the work of the Holy Spirit, the good news about Jesus can be taken to the whole world. Over the centuries of human history, many have been brought to Jesus and have stepped out of darkness into the glorious sunshine of the love of God (John 14:17–26; 16:13).

This was vividly demonstrated on the Day of Pentecost. The new believers received the Holy Spirit at the moment of their conversion, and they were immediately added "by the Holy Spirit" to the infant church. They began to share in its life and practices and give testimony to their newfound faith. The process continued with the next batch of new believers, and the church began to grow rapidly.

This was to be the birth of a whole new society of people. They were different, but not just in the way that they lived. The early Christians and their spiritual descendants, right up to the present day, have not been content merely to know *about* God, but they have desired to know the living God in an intimate personal *relationship*. True Christians do not just gain head knowledge through the words in a book, nor is their experience secondhand. The church was unique because for the first time there was the birth of a society that would never lose any of its members through death. The church will last for eternity.

The Holy Spirit was constantly active in empowering this new community for its mission, equipping the church for its ministry. He was given not just to bless us, but also to make us a blessing to others. He does not deal with us just as individuals, but also as part of a corporate whole. He is not concerned just with current situations, but He wants to prepare us for eternity. His primary desire is to fulfill the heart and intentions of Jesus.

WHY IS THE CHURCH SO IMPORTANT?

Jesus' primary goal on the earth was to gain a people for Himself who would be His gift of love to His Father, and the church has always been at the very heart of the intentions of Jesus for this world.

Many Christians find some areas of church life boring or difficult. But when we view the church through the eyes of Jesus, our perspective changes. Many things can be wrong or awry in a local church, but it still remains the body of believers for whom Jesus died. The church lies at the core of everything for which Jesus lived and died. He clearly revealed His intentions when He boldly proclaimed, "I will build my church, and the gates of Hades will not overcome it" (Matt. 16:18).

Many of us face negative views of the church—either from others or from ourselves! But Jesus specifically brought His church into existence. He ordained it, He commissioned it, and

He intends that it be the express revelation of His glory. We were designed to be *His* church. We can never achieve this separately, only together. The Christian faith is inescapably corporate. Scripture points to "this one" people of God as "the church," and this international family is what Jesus died to bring about. No matter our race, class, education, gender, background, or country of origin, we are all sinners for whom Jesus Christ has died (Rom. 3:23; 8:32). Now we are to live as those for whom He has a great and wonderful purpose. Because we are now part of the church, the Holy Spirit is able to work within our lives so that we might become the servants, children, ambassadors, witnesses, and even the friends of Jesus (1 Pet. 2:16; John 1:12; 2 Cor. 5:20; Acts 1:8; John 15:15). But we can only qualify to fit into these categories through an association with our other brothers and sisters in Christ. We have *all* become believers, not as the result of any good deeds that we have performed, but through the grace and kindness of crucified love. This has been true for each one of us, and we are therefore "all one in Christ Jesus" (Gal. 3:28). Unlikely as it may seem, we really were made for one another!

This principle is plainly revealed in Scripture, and it formed the basis of Jesus' heart cry to His Father in John 17. Four times He pleaded with His Father that all of His disciples "might be one." He longed that we would love and support each other, not just to ensure the survival of the church, but because it was in the will of His Father.

The church should be a clear demonstration of God's love. He has not left us to struggle through on our own; He has given us a family. The church lies at the very core of God's action plan, at the heart of His eternal purposes. When God intends to act within the world, He will do so through His church.

A LIFE-CHANGING CHURCH!

It was said of the early Christians that other people could recognize that they had been with Jesus. But such occurrences were not limited to that place and time.

Few people could have predicted that Albania would provide one of the most outstanding demonstrations of the church in action in the twentieth century. Situated in the Balkans, on the Adriatic coast, and adjoining Montenegro, Macedonia, Greece, and Kosovo, Albania was the poorest and least developed country in Europe. More than forty years of Communist rule had caused devastation in this small country for many decades. For over forty years, dictator Enver Hoja had, in effect, locked up Albania and thrown away the key.

The problems afflicting Albania were more than just economic. Spiritually the nation had endured genuine hardship and loss. But thanks in part to the efforts of one American missionary and his colleagues, there was a small cluster of evangelical congregations in Albania when the Communists came to power. But by the time the Communist reign was over, there were only five Christians remaining. From this handful of survivors, God would rebuild His church. By 1999, none of the original five survivors were still alive, but eight thousand evangelical believers had taken their place in that small nation.[1]

At that precise moment in time, half a million Kosovar Muslim refugees poured across the border into Albania. It would have been so easy for the Albanian Christians to reject these people. They came from the wrong religion, culture, and income bracket. But these young churches began to vividly demonstrate the principles given by Jesus Christ two thousand years ago. They put Christian love into action!

World Relief worked with the Albanian churches to develop a refugee camp in the small southern town of Korce. We did what we could with what we had, but some of the facilities left a lot to be desired. The restrooms in the camp were certainly no exception! While they offered little more than the most primitive of facilities, we did try to maintain them in a reasonably clean and orderly fashion.

Much of the work that had to be done in these latrines was to remove dirty sheets of toilet paper and clean up the residue of human vomit and excreta. Every day one little elderly woman would travel from her home to the camp and work patiently at these extremely unpleasant tasks. Eventually some of the Kosovar Muslims cornered her and demanded to know how much we were paying her for doing such a dirty job. I can still remember her reply: "They don't pay me anything. I am just a volunteer. I do this because I love Jesus."

When the crisis was over and the Serbs had conceded defeat, the Kosovars began the long journey back to their burned-out houses, ruined crops, and destroyed property. But this time they did not travel alone. A number of Albanian Christians declared that they were going back with them. They declared that the refugees were a part of their family, and they would work together to rebuild their homes and reconstruct their shattered lives.

This is the church of Jesus Christ in action, a visible reminder of the fact that we were never intended to stand alone. The Christian faith does not only consist of what an individual thinks or believes, but it also has a clear and visible expression in their daily life. It has sometimes been said that actions speak louder than words, but it took the Albanian church to teach me the truth of that statement. The church is only the true church when the Holy Spirit empowers it to be the church in action.

15

THE HOLY SPIRIT
AND THE CHURCH

How many of us have occasionally been asked for directions to the local church in our city or town? If we think about it, that is an interesting question—and the correct answer would be to say "everywhere." In every individual community where the Holy Spirit has brought people to new life in Jesus Christ, you will find an individual local church that bears His name, a part of the glorious church of Jesus Christ worldwide.

Hopefully most of us have outgrown the misconception that the word *church* refers to a colonial-style building located on a neighboring street corner. The church refers to the people of God, not bricks and mortar! But many of us still view the church as the fellowship we receive in our own locality. In other words, we may understand the local church as being important for our time here on earth, but the worldwide church is a concept reserved for eternity. Too often we have fallen into the trap of making the bride of Christ too small!

The variety of God's family is truly astonishing. Its members have been drawn not only from every kindred, tribe, and nation, but also from every class, culture, and generation. It requires the express design and purpose of the living God to bring such a disparate and unlikely group together to live as His people. Yet we often live in total ignorance of the needs and situations that confront the vast majority of our spiritual brothers and sisters today.

The Holy Spirit and the Church

One definition of the church is, "the community of all those in whom the Holy Spirit dwells." In other words, it consists of all those who have the Spirit (Rom. 8:14–16). The true universal church embraces all those who are children of God, because we share the same heavenly Father (1 Cor. 12:13; Eph. 4:4).

FROM THE SPIRIT—A BRIDE

If the "bride," or church, is fractured and disjointed by national or ethnic distinctions, the Lord could arrive at the altar to marry His bride, only to be greeted by an arm rolling up the aisle, followed by a leg, a couple of fingers, and then an ear or some other section of anatomy! Imagine the confusion as all the various parts desperately try to join themselves together into a bride who would be fit and appropriate for a king.

It seems that some of us who are part of the church in the United States seem to believe that we are the torso of the body, and that everyone else should fit in around us. This is a tragic misrepresentation of the way things should be. We should realize that our common family bond in Jesus transcends any distinction of gender, social standing, racial distinction or even nationality.

There won't be any "American" Christians in heaven—or any British ones either! There won't be African Christians, North American or Asian ones—there will only be family members! It would be good if, when we reach heaven, none of us had to apologize for a neglect of churches and "family members" outside of our own country, especially when we have been entrusted with an abundance of resources that others need so desperately. How much more terrible it would be if our failure to recognize their need turned out to be a matter of life and death! It would be far better if, when we reach heaven, there was only a time of mutual thanksgiving and gratitude.

Sarah lives in Zimbabwe. We met during the painful agonies of the recent famine, and I learned she was a very sincere Christian. A widow, she lives with her five children in the small town of Chikombedze. Seeing her distressed condition and knowing she had no food to give her children, I asked what message I should carry back to her brothers and sisters in the United States.

She began in a way that I would have predicted: "Please tell my brothers and sisters that we are hungry and that the children are starving." But then suddenly she stopped herself. "No, don't tell them that. My brothers and sisters have problems of their own. Tell them a little of what you have seen, but then tell them that the Lord will provide for us."

It was a simple lesson in faith, but it came from thousands of miles away. Yes, the Lord *will* provide, and in recent years I have realized that my own faith has become far too narrow, limited, and parochial. I have had to repent for rejecting the ways in which God was actively moving in the world outside of where I was living. It was not that I was hostile to my brothers and sisters overseas, nor did I object to the initiatives taken on their behalf. It was just that I did not view their problems as my own. I was wrong.

Wherever God is at work in this world, He requires our full cooperation. His activity will never be limited in any way by our acquiescence, approval, or direct involvement. But He would not be happy to discover that His people were paying no attention to what His Spirit was doing in the world. Whether we do so out of conscious neglect or just ignorance is not the issue. The result—the suffering and need of our brothers and sisters—is the same.

We have been given one simple task in the earth—we have been called upon to live as the hands and feet of Jesus.

WHY IS THE CHURCH HERE?

Is this why we are here?

Within my generation there has emerged a real desire to possess "cultural relevance" in the church today. It is good to recognize when an individual has encountered Jesus, but what about the institution to which he or she will then belong? Is it relevant to life in the "real world" of the twenty-first century?

The idea of "total separation" from the world emerged in many twentieth-century evangelical churches. This caused a number of changes to take place, and instead of Christian maturity being measured by the impact an individual had on society, it came to be viewed in terms of the degree to which one withdrew from society. It was almost as if involvement in the local community would inevitably cause contamination by it. Far from the belief that light exterminates darkness, the fearful belief that darkness could extinguish the light took hold of the church in America.

If this were true at a local level, it became even more obvious in international matters. What would appear to be vital issues such as global poverty, economic exploitation, or human rights became seen as "unspiritual." They were regarded more as areas of concern for government or society; they were too "worldly" for the church to become involved in them. Evangelicals seemed to feel that they could become "contaminated" if they moved beyond the safety of their own comfort zones.

Some felt that too great an involvement in social issues could result in Christians being diverted from their "real" task of preaching the gospel—yet it was Christians around the world who were condemned by this neglect to be the victims of starvation, persecution, slavery, or injustice. Some evangelical Christians only gave the impression of being busy in their own church activities where they could feel safe, secure, and unchallenged.

During the 1970s a new congregation started up in London, England, and it called itself "The Invisible Church." I had the opportunity of preaching there on several occasions. They were a great group of people, but I must confess to having a little difficulty with the name they had chosen for themselves. Of course, it is true that all committed Christians are part of a vast body of believers that will only be fully revealed in eternity, and in that sense, we are certainly part of an "invisible" church. But while we are still here on earth, our role is very different.

Jesus told His disciples that they were to be the "light of the world." He instructed all of us to "let your light shine before men, that they may see your good deeds and praise your Father in heaven" (Matt. 5:16). Lamps are not designed to be concealed;

they are designed to be placed on public display so they can fulfill their purpose. In exactly the same way, we are called to shine as lights in our world so that others may be attracted to Jesus. To speak of ourselves as the "invisible" church would, in this sense, be a contradiction in terms!

We must be careful about the way we separate ourselves from the world. Clearly there are habits, activities, friendships, and pastimes to which the Holy Spirit may call a halt.

But while we are not called to be "of" the world, it is undoubtedly true that we are called to remain "in" it. Jesus continually enraged the religious establishment of His day by spending time with the most unsavory members of society. In fact, Jesus never was very fussy about the initial character of those with whom He spent time. He had not come to reinforce the *religious* habits of His age, but instead He came to bring about a revolution of love and to usher in a whole new society on earth. Jesus had come to build His church!

Someone once observed, "I am far within the mark when I say that all the armies that ever marched, and all the navies that were ever built, and all the parliaments that ever sat and all the kings that ever reigned, put together, have not affected the life of man upon the earth as powerfully as has this one solitary life."[1]

Our responsibility is not to simply survive the world and one day enjoy the privileges of heaven. Once we have discovered Jesus, we have no right to keep Him to ourselves. Our God-given task is to reveal His love to those who have yet to meet Him. Although this is easy to say, it is much harder to put into practice.

Many of us would prefer a faith that only demanded our attendance at weekly meetings, the performance of regular devotions, and the avoidance of extreme immorality. But that is not what it means to be a disciple of Jesus. Becoming a Christian does not simply tack Bible-reading, praying, churchgoing, and avoiding a whole string of "do nots" onto our old lifestyle. The implications of being a follower of Christ are far more radical! In fact, the standards are so far beyond mere human abilities that the Holy Spirit has been given to us in order to meet them. And true Christians are not just happy and holy—they are useful as well.

WHAT SHOULD THE CHURCH BE DOING?

Above all, the church is called to make a difference in this world. For this reason the Spirit has come to make us salt and light within our society. These are the twin demands that Jesus lays upon us all (Matt. 5:13–16). We cannot choose between them for the two are inextricably intertwined in God's purposes for His people. If, by His grace, we are to change our world, then we cannot choose the one that appeals the most to us and ignore the other. The two are a combined package; evangelistic proclamation and social demonstration are not to be divorced from each other.

It is interesting to note that "salt" precedes "light," for that is often God's way. Salt acts as a fertilizer and a detergent; it prepares the way for the light, which will conquer the darkness. John affirmed that darkness can never "understand" (or "overcome") the light that comes from God (John 1:5). When the light is at work, it will illuminate further areas that still require cleansing and change.

To have social action without the gospel message would accomplish little more than the puny efforts of secular humanism. But taken the other way around, we are left with the barren emptiness of words without deeds. In the Sermon on the Mount, Jesus taught the significance of both and the strategic importance of their standing together. We must be very careful never to allow our own prejudices, traditions, or preferences to take precedence over the Master's instructions.

God satisfies those who "hunger and thirst for righteousness." Such spiritual hunger and thirst are characteristics of all God's people because our primary desires are spiritual, not material. While nonbelievers are engrossed in the pursuit of possessions, Christians are to be different. Our quest is for God's kingdom and righteousness; that is what we are instructed to "seek first" (Matt. 6:33).

This righteousness is to have a twofold application. First, it is to be moral, in that our lives are to display a character and a conduct that

117

please God. Jesus' "new and improved" instructions concerning murder, reconciliation, legal action, adultery, divorce and remarriage, oaths, revenge, and hatred now go way beyond the Old Testament requirements. (See Matthew 5:21–48.) It is not only in our deeds that our righteousness must be worked out, but also in our thoughts and attitudes.

It would be wrong to assume that we can confine our righteousness merely to the level of a private and personal affair. Biblical righteousness must always include social righteousness. We must become concerned about our integrity in business dealings and family affairs. We must stand with those facing personal victimization, combat injustice both at home and abroad, defend those who are weak and vulnerable, give support to the disadvantaged, and seek to bring freedom to the victims of oppression. In these ways, Christians are committed to the hunger for righteousness in the whole community, and this is pleasing to a righteous God.

CHANGE FROM ABOVE

The Holy Spirit seeks to bring transforming change and renewal into the life of the local church. Sometimes we are guilty of falling into the tempting trap of keeping the Holy Spirit for our own enjoyment. To reduce the Holy Spirit's activities to such a selfish level is to make a tragic mistake.

What are the Holy Spirit's ambitions for the local church? If we seriously want answers this question, we can find them in Scripture. We could simply follow the model of the Jerusalem church. It represents an early effective model of what the church ought to look like, for the early Christians were less preoccupied with the personal blessings they received; they were concerned with other things such as:

Being free from social discrimination

The early church included people from all levels of society. Even Gentiles were included after the Jerusalem Council. The rich, the poor, and the middle class all worshiped together. Mary owned a large house (Acts 12:12–17). Barnabas, Simon of Cyrene, and Ananias and Sapphira were all property owners. But the church also included widows, beggars, invalids, and those from the lower classes. Many were clearly from the middle class; Zebedee, the father of James and John, was sufficiently well off to have employed other workers in the family fishing business. But while these social distinctions were clearly there, they seem to have been of little significance to these early believers. And that is how it should be, for James was to write that in Christ the poor are rich in faith (James 2:5).

Demonstrating their concern for each other

Not only was discrimination absent in the early church, but the believers learned what it meant to share their material possessions with one another.

Spreading the good news of the kingdom

This Christian community was a large church from the outset, but it took an integrated approach to mission. Open-air preaching, personal witnessing, and faith under fire all combined to provide a powerful explanation of the lifestyle they lived and the Jesus they served. All of Jerusalem soon was aware of what was happening (Acts 5:28).

Caring for the poor

All Jews accepted as part of their faith the need to demonstrate compassion and share their resources with the poor. But evidently in the first century this was not happening as it should. By their deep concern for the poor, the Jerusalem church demonstrated the love and mission of Christ. Their involvement included:

- Care for widows and orphans
- Appointing leaders to the administration of social programs
- Healing the sick
- Voluntarily surrendering property
- Common meals and shared housing

- A variety of forms of direct evangelism
- Daily distribution of food

Their own verdict on their efforts was that "there were no needy persons among them" (Acts 4:34).

Jesus had preached and demonstrated justice for the poor, and the early Christians were obedient to His demands. Already the Jerusalem church was putting His principles into practice. It is not surprising that a concern for the poor remained a hallmark of the early Christians (Acts 9:36; 10:4; James 1:27–2:4). And God never forgets the generosity of His people. When a famine struck, Paul organized emergency relief. Those who had given so generously would then receive (Rom. 15:25–27; Gal. 2:10).

Do you feel as uncomfortable as I do when confronted with such an incredible model to follow? Too often we are guilty of confining the operation of the Holy Spirit to the cozy, privatized area of our own local church and the needs that we have close to home. Jesus wants to do something far more radical. He wants to take what He has done in our individual and church lives and use it as a launching pad to challenge and transform our world.

It is a sobering question to face up to honestly, but if we compare our lifestyle to the lifestyle of the Jerusalem church, how would we measure up? Is Jesus alive and well and operating freely in your church—and mine? Or have we stopped short and gotten stuck somewhere between the realities of Calvary and a genuine Pentecost?

LIVING BY THE SPIRIT

One minor league soccer team had become a bit of a joke. At one stage in a particularly disastrous season, there were less than six games left, and they hadn't won yet! The problem was that losing had grown to be so familiar and they had become so accustomed to failure that winning became inconceivable.

That same sense of failure can often result in burnout in our Christian lives. Time and again we may act in good faith, responding to calls of the Spirit for a deeper commitment, only to fail again. Promises, resolutions, and good intentions all to seem to be to no avail. I once heard actress Glenda Jackson make the comment, "I don't mind people telling me how awful I am, providing they offer me a lifeline to help me to be better....But no one ever does."

Jesus was completely different. He faced all the trials and temptations of life, yet He remained totally consistent in following His Father's will.

A PERFECT LIFE

Throughout His time on earth, Jesus lived in complete obedience to the will of His Father, and by doing so He initiated a totally new era. He illustrated all those principles that God longed to birth within His own people.

A new direction

Jesus took His orders from the Holy Spirit. We read in Luke's Gospel, "Jesus...was led by the Spirit into the desert" to be tempted there by Satan (Luke 4:1). The Spirit did not simply direct Jesus to the desert and then dump Him; Jesus went into the desert full of the Spirit, and He emerged in the power of the Spirit. The Holy Spirit not only guided Jesus into God's way, but He also equipped Him to deal with each situation. By following God's directive Spirit, Jesus received all that He needed to defeat Satan's temptation and to stride ahead into His life's work.

A new authority

It took a Roman centurion to recognize that a life lived in complete submission to God's direction possessed an authority that the world had never seen before. "Just say the word, and my servant will be healed. For I myself am a man under authority, with soldiers under me. I tell this one, 'Go,' and he goes," he said (Luke 7:7–8). No one responded to the centurion because of his own authority—it was the delegated power that he received through the Roman military chain of command that made the difference. In the same way, when we enjoy a life in the Spirit and come under His divine direction, we begin to know what it means to live under the authority of God Himself.

A new obedience

Jesus followed only where the Spirit led Him, and that is why He could confidently assert to His Father, "I have finished the work you gave me to do" (John 17:4, GNT). Jesus did exactly what His Father required, as the Spirit revealed it to Him. Jesus provided us with the perfect example of a life lived under the authority and in the power of the Holy Spirit, not human endeavor. That kind of obedience is required from us as well.

A PROPER DIVISION

In his letter to the Thessalonian church, Paul outlined the structure of man when he asked that God would "keep your whole being—spirit, soul and body" (1 Thess. 5:23, GNT). The writer of the Book of Hebrews also spoke of the soul and the spirit (Heb. 4:12).

This does not mean that men and women are made up of three separate parts that we could take apart and lay side by side on a table. You will never see a disembodied soul making an ethereal response to an altar call! Scripture demonstrates that our body, soul, and spirit represent three different aspects of our being that are intimately bound together. Each fulfills a different function on behalf of the others, and together they represent our ability to respond and operate in different areas.

The body provides our contact with the outside world through the five senses: taste, smell, hearing, sight, and touch. Our spirit provides contact with God through communing with Him, discerning His will, and allowing His creativity to operate through us. The soul is the seat of our emotions, our intellect, and our will. It is our will that acts as a valve, determining the degree to which we will be controlled by God's Spirit.

Many who have no commitment to Jesus Christ have yet made the intellectual and emotional decision to imitate His purity, humility, and love. They have tried to do this by their own efforts, and many have even done a pretty good job of it. But God wants His people to enjoy a totally new dimension of life, not just an imitation. We are not just called to copy Jesus but to actually partake of His nature so that the Holy Spirit may radiate the glory of God through our lives. It may be hard to tell the imitation from the real thing, but one is the product of human effort while the other is a divine initiative.

Tragically, many Christians fall into the same trap. We try by our own efforts to do the Holy Spirit's job for Him, often with pitiful results. Andrew Murray has suggested that both the church and individual Christians must dread the "inordinate activity of the soul."[1] The proud mind and intrusive will of man can create the most dreadful hindrance to spiritual maturity.

Many Christians are content with where they are. For many, it is more than sufficient to be respected by their neighbors and to live upright, kind, compassionate, and orthodox Christian lives. Too often they try to find God through their own intellect, to respond to Him with their own emotions, and to serve Him as an act of their own will. But before we can know God, respond to Him, or serve Him, we first need to allow His Spirit to breathe new life into our spirits. Then our mind, emotions, and will are driven by, motivated by, and submitted to the life of the Spirit of God.

We need to be controlled by the Spirit. It is not enough to determine within our souls—our mind, will, and emotions—that we will follow Christ. We must allow the whole of our lives to be guided by our spirit and our capacity to receive the Holy Spirit, to love God, and to live in His strength, not our own.

It can be crushing and humiliating to realize that we have performed actions that were good when judged by our standards but were not in the purpose and intention of God. Even after overcoming basic sin, our spiritual battle has only just begun, and early victories come only with the Holy Spirit's help. Our ongoing struggle cannot be carried on in our own strength. "Are you so foolish? After beginning with the Spirit, are you now trying to attain your goal by human effort?" (Gal. 3:3).

We can be so well intentioned but so dreadfully wrong. That is why Jesus repeated one instruction on so many occasions and why the Holy Spirit inspired the Gospel writers to record it seven times: the life controlled by personal ambitions, desires, decisions, and activities must die to itself. "Whoever finds his life will lose it, and whoever loses his life for my sake will find it" (Matt. 10:39; 16:25; Mark 8:35; Luke 9:24; 14:26; 17:33; John 12:25).

The Greek word for *soul* could be translated *life*. Jesus' point is that lives lived for personal ends and in our own strength are futile. Once we give up our self-centered lifestyles and concentrate on living in the power of the Spirit, our lives will become profitable and gain eternal value.

Living by the Spirit

A PRECIOUS DESTINY

Jesus freely confessed that "the Son can do nothing by himself.... By myself I can do nothing" (John 5:19, 30). Never satisfied with just going about doing good, Jesus always waited for His Father's best. He waited until the Spirit would move. He even delayed His ministry, spending eighteen years in a carpenter's workshop waiting on the Holy Spirit.

The hours Jesus spent in prayer with His Father were to ensure that "not my will, but yours be done" (Luke 22:42).

While we rush around doing this or that for the Lord, we should learn from Jesus. He waited, listened, and then allowed the Holy Spirit to equip and direct Him. Without this kind of commitment, our self-motivated dedication will generate "good" things, but things that will never amount to more than wood, grass, or straw.

It is only as we place our mind, emotions, and will completely at the disposal of the Holy Spirit that our labors can have any value. Only as we first listen to the voice of the Master Builder will anything of value be created. As we place each well-intentioned activity in the hands of Jesus, we must relinquish it. We are called to act under orders. We must not accept the perverted logic of this age, which assumes that once we have seen a need we have received God's call. It is only what God places in our hands to perform that should demand our time or effort. As day by day we surrender to the direction of the Holy Spirit, we can go about our Father's business with confidence, knowing that we are not going alone.

The apostle Paul examined his failures and assessed his life in this way:

> Those who live as their human nature tells them to, have their minds controlled by what human nature wants. Those who live as the Spirit tells them to, have their minds controlled by what the Spirit wants. To be controlled by human nature results in death; to be controlled by the Spirit results in life and peace.
>
> —ROMANS 8:5–6, GNT

Paul saw a simple answer to human failure: "If by the Spirit you put to death the misdeeds of the body, you will live" (v. 13).

And that is what led Paul to his ultimate conclusion. He affirmed that "those who are led by the Spirit of God are sons of God. For you did not receive a spirit that makes you a slave again to fear, but you received the Spirit of sonship" (vv. 14–15).

It is only as He works out His purposes within our lives that we begin to discover our destiny, to know what we were made to be— sons of God, His own children, full of confidence that He will perform His purposes in us both here and throughout eternity.

To experience God at work in our lives is not a one-time event but a consistent laying down of our lives for His service. Such surrender has to be a day-by-day experience. And in this process, I have learned to appreciate the bumper sticker that says: "Please be patient. God isn't finished with me yet!"

ANOINTED—FOR WHAT?

E very day, we are witnesses to the saving love of Jesus and the transforming power of His Spirit in our lives. We can only live and speak as the Spirit enables us. But God also intends His people to demonstrate His power in the world. He calls us to specific acts of ministry and service, which at times demand a special empowering from the Holy Spirit.

Throughout the Old Testament, we read about the Holy Spirit "coming upon" people to prepare them for service. In the New Testament the Holy Spirit comes to live "within" all of God's people.

This distinction between the Holy Spirit coming "in" or "on" a person is not a completely rigid one. The Holy Spirit came "on" the 120 believers on the Day of Pentecost, and it was in the authority of that anointing that they then moved out and turned their world upside down.

The Holy Spirit may well live "within" us from day to day, but He still comes "upon" us as He anoints our lives for particular acts of service. While His presence within us is permanent, His anointing that comes upon us is not. Four times we read that the Spirit of God came "on" Samson (Judg. 13:25; 14:6, 19; 15:14). But then came the fateful day when "he did not know that the Lord had left him" (Judg. 16:20). Through his disobedience and lack of commitment he had lost the power of the Spirit.

King Saul also forfeited his anointing. David, who succeeded Saul as the king of Israel, was panic-stricken when his adultery with Bathsheba and subsequent murder of her husband was exposed. He was terrified at the thought that the same could happen to him. That is why he pleaded with God, "Do not...take your Holy Spirit from me" (Ps. 51:11).

Without the anointing of the Holy Spirit, our labors for God will never attain their greatest potential. Day by day we need the Holy Spirit's filling and anointing on our lives. Then and only then can we join Jesus in saying:

> The Spirit of the Lord is on me, because he has anointed me to preach good news to the poor. He has sent me to proclaim freedom for the prisoners and recovery of sight for the blind, to release the oppressed, to proclaim the year of the Lord's favor.
>
> —LUKE 4:18–19

ANOINTED TO LIVE A NEW LIFE

At this point many new believers encounter incredible difficulties. It is great to be saved and know that we are going to heaven, but what are we going to do in the meantime? What is this new life we are to lead, and how is the Holy Spirit involved in it?

The easiest way to respond to this question is that, in effect, we have been delivered from one lifestyle and culture and transplanted into another. On the other hand, the Bible clearly teaches that we have been called to continue living within the world, not escape from it. Our witness to others is important, and the evidence of our changed lives should encourage others to respond to the call of God's love.

Rather than relaxing in self-satisfied contentment after we have been saved, we should be constantly striving to share with others that same saving grace that we have encountered in Jesus so that they too can joyfully receive the same forgiveness, release, and life-giving Holy Spirit that we have discovered. In other words, God's blessings have not only been given to us for our own comfort and enjoyment. They have been given for us to share them with others. As the English Archbishop William Temple once observed, "The church is the only human society that exists for the benefits of its non-members."[1]

Second Corinthians 6:17 reads, "Come out from among them, and be ye separate, saith the Lord" (KJV). Too many Christians have used this as an excuse to not maintain any contact with unbelievers. But that is not what this verse means! We should be a holy people, set apart for God's purposes, but we need to always remember that we have not been reborn just for ourselves, to stay cloistered away from the rest of the world. The Holy Spirit wants to work in us and through us to draw others to the Father. Our faith is not a "just-me-and-Jesus-together-in-a-cozy-huddle" kind of faith, but it is a faith that is intended to be shared.

Christianity is an *inclusive* religion, not an *exclusive* one. Unfortunately, because we have failed to grasp this truth, we have become submerged within our own subculture of "Christian" activities, entertainment, and programs. The tragic result is that outside of its walls, the church is seen as irrelevant, having made little or no constructive contribution to human society.

So many local evangelical churches have lost any sense of corporate responsibility toward the rest of society. Plenty of reasons are given to stay out of the world, but the alternative is never shared: to become an agent of change in the local community.

New converts are often the ones who catch the "vision" first. Full of fresh zeal, enthusiasm, and the Holy Spirit, they often find it difficult to understand why they should keep their newfound faith to themselves. Rather than withdrawing from the world, they seek to transform it!

The anointing of the Holy Spirit equips and empowers us to withstand temptation and to overcome the assaults and rejection of this world. We do not have to cower in a corner or avoid all contact with the world in order to remain pure. Rather, let us represent the cause of Christ to our world and demonstrate our new, changed lives to those who desperately need this change as well.

ANOINTED FOR SUFFERING

As the people of God we have been promised two things: success and suffering. At first, these two promises might seem to contradict each other, but they actually do not. The success that is promised in Scripture relates more to our future than to the present circumstances in which we find ourselves. Because our modern world is so dependent on the idea of "instant success," it is no surprise that the idea of a promise of suffering is not enthusiastically received by many Christians. We would prefer to believe that the degree to which we are serving God can be seen by the amount of material blessings we received on earth. In its crudest form, the idea is that our Christianity can somehow be measured by the condition of our physical health and the prosperity of our bank account.

Can we really pretend that such ideas follow the example of the One who denied Himself the security of a home, who possessed so little available cash that He used a conveniently floating fish to pay the tax bill (Matt. 8:20; 17:27)? Jesus Himself was the One to emphasize the demands of sacrificial discipleship. He promised His disciples that they would suffer in His cause, and we certainly have no reason to anticipate an easier ride for our lives today! In fact, author Paul Billheimer once wrote these words that have been a spiritual warning to me through the years:

> The impression is current that to be saved and filled with the Spirit opens a charmed life entirely trouble-free, where all problems are instantaneously solved and where miracles never cease. According to some ... life is one hilarious rollercoaster picnic and lark. No one should ever get sick, or, if he does, he should be healed immediately by simple, effortless faith. If he needs money, all he has to do is ask God for it and the heavens open and down it pours. If anyone does not prosper and live affluently it is simply because he is not spiritually "on the ball."[2]

These ideas have infiltrated into the thoughts and lives of many Christians, often with disastrous consequences, for they cause us to focus our attention upon ourselves.

Jesus introduced us to a concept that may seem foreign to our twenty-first-century way of life: that we ourselves should be prepared to suffer for the sake of others. Nowhere is this more clear than when He said, "Greater love has no one than this, that he lay down his life for his friends" (John 15:13). This is the way that Jesus lived, and we should expect no less of ourselves. If we object that such unselfish living is impossible, we would be right, if we are trying to do it in our own strength. The answer is that the Holy Spirit has been given to empower us!

I don't know exactly how old Irma is, nor do I know the story of how she came to Jesus. I only know that she belongs to Him, because of her response to the tragic events of January 13, 2001. How Irma held to her faith in the face of intense suffering witnessed to all her neighbors of her love for God.

It was around ten thirty in the morning when the earthquake struck. Irma was in her house with two others from the local church. Panic-stricken at the severity of the quake, they grabbed hands, believing in that instant that the end of the world had come. Then they heard the noise, a noise like nothing they had ever heard before. When the second tremor finally stopped, they stepped out of Irma's house and gazed in shock at what remained of their middle-class neighborhood in San Salvador.

Looking up at the thickly wooded hillside that had overshadowed the dwellings just minutes before, they realized with horror that one-third of it was missing! The earthquake had dislodged the hillside, and the trees had come crashing down upon this peaceful and unsuspecting San Salvadorian suburb. Some trees had traveled almost a mile before landing in a kitchen or a bedroom. The rest of the hillside immediately became a landslide, as the dirt and rocks hurtled down to cover what remained of the houses. When the rescuers arrived, the area had become a vast communal graveyard, with survivors milling around in a state of shock. Then there were those such as Irma, whose houses stood on either side of the devastation. These people stepped out of their doorways to survey the ravaged area in horror.

For the survivors, and their friends and neighbors, it was a moment of total confusion. For Irma it was an opportunity, a chance to pray with lost and suffering people and to offer what help and support she could. Many Christians had died, including at least one pastor. Two church buildings were demolished. Irma's pastor, Saul, had lost seven of his congregation, killed in the disaster. But God's people were not thinking of themselves at that time but of the sufferings of others. Survivors such as Irma were ready and willing to get involved, and the distribution of food and clothing was swiftly arranged. Under an anointing from the Lord, Irma was able to minister to the needs of those who had lost everything they possessed, and the end results of what was achieved during that time will only be revealed in eternity.

We are not promised an easy life. The Holy Spirit has come to make us into the hands and feet of Jesus, the One who won us with His "suffering love." He suffered and died to bring us to Himself, and He requires our own self-giving love in return (1 Cor. 13:4). God matures us, His people, and teaches us to share in the sufferings of others, not by providing us with an easy life, but by exposing us to the sorrows and pressures of life. When we discover our own Spirit-given capacity to endure tribulation, we learn what it means to be worthy of God's calling on our lives (Heb. 12:5–11).

The apostle Paul clearly believed that suffering was one strategy the Holy Spirit used to prepare us for the glory that was to come (Rom. 8:18; 2 Cor. 4:17–18). And that is where our "success" comes into play. As A. W. Tozer once remarked, we can afford to suffer here on earth because we will have eternity to enjoy ourselves.[3] We have been called to share in the sufferings of Jesus, but we have also been promised an eternal triumphant reign as the bride of Christ!

ANOINTED FOR BLESSING

While we must remember that we are not immune from the challenges in this life—which the Holy Spirit helps us to overcome—we must not go to the other extreme: that we cannot be blessed in the here and now. Some of us naïvely expect that all things will be automatically perfect for the people of God, and this, we have seen is incorrect. But we must maintain a balance, knowing that we will suffer in this world, but that the Holy Spirit also brings an anointing to bless.

The early Christian ascetic Simon Stylites condemned himself to living for almost forty years on top of a pillar. He did this because he viewed personal hardship as a basic part of the Christian life, and he believed that nothing was more important than to keep himself untainted, separated from the evils of a sin-sick world.

The ancient Greek world saw suffering as a virtue in itself. That is not the Christian way, for we are called to suffer *for a purpose*: to extend the kingdom of God. Suffering must never be regarded as an end in itself; God only allows it because He wants to mature and ultimately bless His people.

Whether or not Simon Stylites was right to live on top of a pillar is not for us to judge. What we must recognize is that God will provide us with all that we need to live our lives for Him, even though His estimation of what we need may not always agree with our own!

In the 1990s, many of God's people experienced a number of "new" and exciting blessings. The ministry of the "Kansas City prophets," the visits of John Wimber, and the arrival of the "Toronto Blessing" all became much-discussed topics in the charismatic world. Visits from Australian bishops and evangelical leaders created much excitement in non-charismatic circles, but because these visits were more "intellectual," they caused very little controversy. The same could not be said of the more experiential encounters, such as the "Toronto Blessing."

Christians seem to love to disagree with each other! In our eagerness to defend our own understanding of the truth, we spend our time fiercely debating the merits of our case and the errors of those who disagree with us. This was the case with the "Toronto Blessing" and other outpourings that have taken place. The truth is, many of our brothers and sisters received a fresh release of the Holy Spirit at those meetings. Many found refreshment at a time when their spiritual lives appeared to be arid and dry. One friend of mine was facing a difficult period in his life at that time. He received prayer, but he did not burst into spontaneous laughter or fall over backward; he simply rocked gently from side to side, feeling cradled in the loving arms of Jesus. It was an incredibly comforting experience for him.

I will never forget the words of a reporter who said that he was not aware that laughing in church had been declared by ecclesiastical authorities to be a venal sin! Perhaps it takes the sane words of that Jewish commentator to bring some perspective. While we spend our time quibbling about the spiritual experiences of one another, brothers and sisters in Christ around the world face suffering, persecution, and death. How we fail to see the real issues at times!

The mistaken zeal and misplaced priorities of the church led me to write a book some years ago. It was in an angrier vein, entitled *With a Church Like This, Who Needs Satan?* When God wants to bless His people, He follows no man-made prescription, and we should be ready to receive absolutely any blessing that He wants to shower upon us. What often proves to be more difficult is to rejoice with others when the Lord chooses to bless them but denies the blessing to us.

ANOINTED TO HEAL

Many years ago, I was about to conduct a coffee-bar mission in a London suburb. While praying with a group of local Christians on the morning before the mission was to begin, we were suddenly interrupted. A young nurse entered the room in tears. She had been longing to be involved in the mission, but just that morning her doctor had confirmed that she had perforated her eardrum. She would be unable to hear well enough in a coffee-bar atmosphere to share her faith.

I can't explain why I reacted so strongly, except that I knew that this was not what God wanted. I urged one of the youth leaders to stand with me and pray for the girl. Never before had I specifically prayed for healing for anyone. But she was healed! The youth leader was as surprised as I was, but he took things one step further—he married her!

Healing was very important in the ministry of Jesus, but why? The Scriptures provide several reasons.

Healing was an expression of the mind and will of God for humankind.

Mark records the moment when "a man with leprosy came to him and begged him on his knees, 'If you are willing, you can make me clean.' Filled with compassion, Jesus reached out his hand and touched the man. 'I am willing,' he said. 'Be clean!'" (Mark 1:40–41).

Healing was a sign of the deep compassion and love of Jesus.

The Greek word Mark uses for *pity* is often used of the compassion of Jesus, and it indicates a love that flows from the very depths of a man or woman. This is no surface reaction or response; it is a heartfelt compassion, what could genuinely be called a "gut-level" sort of love.

Healing was a fulfillment of prophecy.

"This was to fulfill what was spoken through the prophet Isaiah, 'He took our infirmities and carried our diseases'" (Matt. 8:17).

Healing brings glory to God.

"He is blind so that God's power might be seen at work in him" (John 9:3, GNT).

Healing stimulates faith.

"Believe me when I say that I am in the Father and the Father is in me; or at least believe on the evidence of the miracles themselves" (John 14:11).

DESCENDING LIKE A DOVE

It is amazing to see the changes that physical healing can introduce! Michael Cassidy shares the following account:

> When I finally reached Chicago some weeks later, Lawrence Hammond greeted me warmly and told me his story. As I remember it at this time, it went something like this. He had been taken terribly ill with some kind of intestinal blockage and other problems. This landed him in the hospital where his condition deteriorated horribly. His tummy had blown up to the size of a football and was grotesquely swollen.
>
> The surgery which was decided upon did not apparently give much ground for hope. Having insisted on knowing his true condition, he had been told his chances were slender.
>
> "I think they were mainly interested in me as a guinea pig for medical science," he said and laughed.
>
> Anyway, he decided to call his Episcopal minister to come to his bedside to anoint him with oil and pray over him. This was two or three days before the operation.
>
> He waited patiently, but desperation mounted as no minister appeared. Finally, the day the operation was to take pace, the new curate who had just come to their church arrived in a state of jitters at his bedside.
>
> "I'm terribly sorry," he apologized, as he put his hat down on the bed, "Rector is out of town and can't come, so they asked me to come over. But I don't know what to do. They never taught us about healing at Seminary, and I've never anointed with oil, and I don't know what to do."
>
> "My heart absolutely sank," Lawrence said to me. "I had set so much store by a visit from our minister as I knew he believed in healing. Now here I was with this poor young fellow, quite lost and at sea."
>
> "Well," he went on, knowing he had me all goggle-eyed and transfixed, "I simply asked the curate if he believed God could heal, to which he replied in the affirmative. Then I asked him to lay hands on me and pray. The little

fellow, almost ashen in color, reached out his hands towards my bulging stomach. Then as he touched me and before he could pray it was as if a 3,000-volt electric current went through me. The curate got such a fright he rebounded from the bed and literally fell to the ground, knocking his hat off as he did so. And there and then the physical swelling of my stomach visibly subsided, like air coming out of a balloon or a soccer ball."

Lawrence's face glowed as he told the story. "So I pulled all the plastic tubes out of myself and leaped from my bed shouting 'I've been healed, I've been healed!' By this time the little curate was up off the ground, and we sort of danced a jig round the ward. All this noise attracted the attention of the Jewish rabbi who was passing the ward. He had often seen me and knew the seriousness of my condition. As he perceived the spectacle and saw my normal-sized stomach and gathered what had happened, he rushed out the door and down the passage shouting 'It's just like the Red Sea! It's just like the Red Sea!'"

So there they all were–the whooping patient, the dancing curate and the ecstatic rabbi–when several horrified nurses rushed in calling for order, calm and sanity.

"But he's been healed," beamed the curate.

"Yes, he has, he has, he has," bubbled the rabbi.

Anyway, the nurses, now joined by a doctor or two, finally got Lawrence back into bed.[4]

Power–for Jesus, for the early church, and for Christians today–is no wild, irrational thing. Obviously we cannot control God, but we do have a certain control over whether or not God's power may work through us. There are conditions that need to be fulfilled in us if the Holy Spirit is to move freely through our lives.

- Our motives must be pure. As Simon the sorcerer discovered, money could not purchase God's power; it is not available for just anyone.

- Prayer and fasting are sometimes the necessary preparation for God to empower His people (Mark 9:29).

- God's power is only available to His people and at His own initiative and intention (Luke 10:9, 21; Acts 5:12).

- All glory and honor must go to God, not to those whom He has used as His servants (Acts 3:9).

- It is important to be grounded in the body of Christ, rightly related to Jesus, to one another, and to our role and function within the body.

We must be careful not to presume that God's intention will be to heal every person on every single occasion. Although healing should remain our expectation and hope, we must be careful to encourage faith, not foolishness. We must first seek to find God's will and then act in obedience to that will rather than our own desires, however good they may be!

Over the years, I have discovered that God's actions are often spontaneous. He rarely chooses to fit into the well-worn pathways that I have carved out for Him. We operate in Jesus' name and only under His authority, and God does not respond to our own pet formulas. *He* tells *us* what to do, not vice versa.

There is real variety in what God does. Healing can be progressive or instantaneous, or God may call His people to endure suffering in order that He might fulfill His purposes. When the disciples tried to claim a monopoly on God's dealings, Jesus rebuked them:

> "Master," said John, "we saw a man driving out demons in your name and we tried to stop him, because he is not one of us." "Do not stop him," Jesus said, "for whoever is not against you is for you."
>
> —LUKE 9:49–50

Anointed—for What?

One final point is that the Lord responds to faith, not familiarity. When He went back to Nazareth Jesus discovered that "only in his hometown, among his relatives and in his own house is a prophet without honor" (Mark 6:4). For that reason, "he could not do any miracles there, except lay his hands on a few sick people and heal them. And he was amazed at their lack of faith" (vv. 5–6).

ANOINTED TO DELIVER

Jesus' strategy was to take one life (His own), and through His living outside Satan's stronghold, He would raise up thousands of others. The authority of His Holy Spirit is for Jesus alone to give: "I have given you authority to trample on snakes and scorpions and to overcome all the power of the enemy; nothing will harm you" (Luke 10:19).

Here are some guidelines for dealing with demonic spirits.

- Never go looking for demons. Don't imagine the demonic where it doesn't exist, but do listen to the voice of your spirit and the witness of others.

- Distinguish carefully between the levels of demonic activity: a person may be demonized, oppressed, or, in very rare cases, possessed.

- Distinguish carefully between psychiatric or psychological disorders, which can be fostered by Satan, and demonic activity.

- Don't act alone. Beware of being impetuous, and don't forget the law!

- Don't lay hands on the demonized person. Rebuke them, speaking in Jesus' name. Note that the vacuum must be filled and the damage healed by the Holy Spirit (Luke 11:25–26).

- Warn fellow Christians to avoid any association at all with areas of occultism, such as horoscopes, psychic arts, séances, and astral projection.

- Do not give credit to Satan, and don't become fascinated or interested in his work, even under the guise of spiritual care. Exalt Jesus; dismiss the devil!

- Avoid wasting time on those who have dabbled in the occult but have no desire to be freed from the results. There are six conditions for freedom to take place: humility, honesty, confession of sin, repentance, forgiveness of all others, and calling on the name of the Lord.

I have hesitated even mentioning this aspect of the Spirit's activity, as we run the grave risk of spreading knowledge that is frankly unhelpful. The great number of books on Satan and his works speaks volumes of the fascination that the subject holds for the people of God. I far prefer the attitude expressed in the title of Michael Green's book: *I Believe in Satan's Downfall*.[5]

ANOINTED TO BRING GOOD NEWS TO THE POOR

The anointing of the Holy Spirit to bring good news to the poor is often overlooked. We would prefer to focus on the more spectacular demonstrations of His power! Yet Jesus came to the world to share His message of hope with ordinary people. Jesus reserved some of His most devastating criticisms for the rich, pointing out that the problems of wealth make it "easier for a camel to go through the eye of a needle than for a rich man to enter the kingdom of God" (Mark 10:25). It is scarcely surprising that the disciples were "even more amazed." No longer were social privilege and income a qualification for spiritual superiority. The fact that the "good news is preached to the poor" was sent as a message by Jesus to John the Baptist to convince him, once and for all, that the Messiah had indeed arrived (Matt. 11:5)!

LOVE ON FIRE!

Many of us often pray the words, "Come, Holy Spirit." Yet I wonder if we are really aware of what we are asking for! Too often we have been content to view the Holy Spirit as just a useful "addition" to our lives.

In John's Gospel, the Holy Spirit is referred to as the Helper, the Counselor, the Comforter, and the Advocate. In fact, He is a combination of all four: an advocate to plead our case, a counselor to guide us, and a helper to assist us with all those things that we could never do alone. But a comforter?

The picture of a "comforter" in biblical times was not that of a sympathetic ear! It can be compared to a picture portrayed on the Bayeux tapestry of the Norman victory in 1066 at the Battle of Hastings. This picture depicts one of Duke William's supporters prodding a reluctant Norman soldier into battle with the point of a spear in his rear. Underneath the picture is the poignant comment that "King William comforteth his soldiers"!

As our Comforter, the Holy Spirit is the One who mobilizes us for battle! His anointing is for the healing of the brokenhearted, the defeat of the enemy, and the proclamation of the gospel to the poor. The apostle Paul assures us that the Spirit is "a deposit guaranteeing our inheritance until the redemption of those who are God's possession" (Eph. 1:14).

THE SPIRIT IN THE WORLD

The last thirty-five years have witnessed an awakening within evangelical Christianity to the social implications of the gospel. Our Lord is concerned with the entire gamut of human life, *both* physical and spiritual. Organizations as diverse as Focus on the Family, World Relief, Evangelicals for Social Action, the Salvation Army, World Vision, and a whole host of others are helping to transform the evangelical landscape and mission of the church in the United States. This new awareness graphically brings to life the significance of the words of Jesus: "You are the light of the world.... that they may see your good deeds and praise your Father in heaven" (Matt. 5:14, 16).

The Holy Spirit is given to be our helper, and He encourages us to meet the needs that exist on our own doorstep. His call affects both what we say and what we do; we speak God's Word into situations, and we get our hands dirty. The call to servanthood, giving, love, and prayer is the message of the Holy Spirit to us as He calls us to be "the Word in working clothes."

Loving our neighbor is not to be left to the welfare system! It is as we visit others and become involved in the life of the community that we spread the true message of Jesus to the poor. As we face the needs of those who suffer from poverty and discrimination, those who lack water, health care, education, or employment, the Holy Spirit issues specific calls on our lives. Those who are elderly, unemployed, refugees, sick, disabled, immigrant, low-wage earners... those who live in overcrowded living conditions... those who are in ethnic minority groups... even those who are not yet born, all need to see the demonstration of the love of Jesus. Only then will the church be seen as a caring and helping body of real people.

David Watson was one of the most well-loved and best-known leaders in the United Kingdom during the early days of the Charismatic movement. He commented from his experience as an Anglican vicar that "evangelism and social action are like the two blades of a pair of scissors: if you have one without the other, you lose your cutting edge."

A simple illustration can be found in the way a number of churches in the United Kingdom have faced the problem of mounting unemployment among young people. Instead of just observing the situation, church premises have been adapted as drop-in centers for the unemployed. Here training can be given in job application and interview procedures. Community enterprise projects and job creation schemes under Christian supervision have been developed. An informal atmosphere provides opportunities for unemployed Christians and non-Christians to relax and work together.

God called His people Israel to be unique, to be an example of social concern. They were to be committed to the refugee, the poor, needy, widowed, and orphaned. They were to rule by justice, peace, and love, with no slaves or elaborate social hierarchy. As God's people today, we need to ask ourselves whether or not we are sufficiently responding to God's call to give to the poor, the elderly, and the disadvantaged.

THE SPIRIT AMONG THE POOR

As an example, conditions in Southern Sudan are hundreds of years behind the rest of the world. Approximately the size the United States east of the Mississippi River, Southern Sudan possesses less than ten miles of paved roads.[1]

The first time I arrived at the remote village of Leithnom in Sudan, our little plane bounced unhappily along what could only be described as an apology for an airstrip. To call it a runway would be exaggerating beyond acceptable limits! Not only was the landing strip primitive, but also the village and its population were clearly suffering. Many exhibited a whole host of symptoms related to chronic malnutrition and serious deprivation.

The first problem we experienced was that we were not expected. They were in the midst of such an extreme famine that most people were simply concentrating on their survival. As I walked through the village, I noticed that about two hundred people had gathered together underneath a spreading tree. Now anyone who knows Africa will appreciate that this usually indicates a religious meeting. I paused to ask the people what they were doing. Their reply was instantaneous.

"We're worshiping Jesus." Then came their immediate question to me: "Have you ever heard of Him?"

No sooner had I replied that I had that their next question followed: "We've heard that there is a Book about Him. Have you ever seen one?"

Before we could address the people's near-starvation and the famine, they insisted that we provide them with Bibles! Perhaps it is no great surprise, then, that a few months later, over one thousand people were baptized from that village and the surrounding area.

After the building of a school, provision of initial veterinary services, training of lay leaders for the emerging church, and construction of a mini-hospital, that same village was systematically and regularly bombed over a period of several weeks by the air force of the Islamic fundamentalist Northern Sudanese government. The primary targets were the church and the World Relief compound.

But in another part of Southern Sudan, the villages in the area of South Bor witnessed the sudden conversion of over 90 percent of the population in a period of just a few weeks.[2] As in Leithnom, it has proved difficult to explain the power of what took place. No visiting evangelist was involved, nor did those areas possess a single church or local pastor. But the absence of a missionary or an evangelistic initiative should not confuse us. The annals of church history are riddled with incidents when the Holy Spirit has chosen to intervene suddenly and sovereignly in human affairs. What makes it even stranger is the way that so often this direct intervention of the Holy Spirit comes on behalf of those who are among the poorest of the poor.

THE SPIRIT OF OBEDIENCE

Jesus was born among the chronically poor, and He urged that we should show love and compassion to those less fortunate than ourselves. Living the Spirit-filled life certainly includes living in obedience to the commands of Jesus.

It is not true that this emphasis was only necessary in Jesus' day; today is His moment as well, and the same needs still apply. About eight hundred million people, one-fifth of the human race, are destitute and lack the basic necessities for survival. More than one billion live on less than one dollar a day.[3]

We are all affected by global problems. Television and radio have removed our ignorance. Besieged by newsreel pictures of the poverty, starvation, and death of thousands each day, we can no longer claim that we are unaware of what is going on. Gross economic inequality is coupled with political oppression, and people are denied fundamental human rights by totalitarian regimes of Left and Right alike. In less extreme circumstances, racial discrimination and sexual discrimination create other societal problems that are often met by a stone wall of Christian apathy. Martin Luther King cried out in the face of such disinterest that, when we arrive at the judgment seat of Jesus Christ, we will have to confess not only the "vitriolic actions and words of the bad people, but also for the appalling silence and apathy of the good people."[4]

Throughout history God has recognized and responded to all kinds of human suffering (Exod. 3:7; Acts 7:34). His great calling on our lives was given in Jesus' great sermon on the Mount of Olives. Jesus urged His people to be "salt for all mankind," but He gave the stern warning, "If the salt loses its saltiness, how can it be made salty again? It is no longer good for anything, except to be thrown out and trampled by men" (Matt. 5:13).

We need to ask whether our generosity stops at the borders of our own country, or does it extend overseas as well. When our brothers and sisters in other parts of the world need our help, we should be happy to demonstrate what it means to belong to another "kingdom," the universal church of God. Evangelical churches in America have the opportunity today to demonstrate that we are truly part of a worldwide family. It is an opportunity that we must not miss, because while we have been blessed with more than 80 percent of the resources that the Lord Jesus has entrusted to His church in the world, we must never forget that He has also called us to be His "banker" and to know what it means to be used!

Are we more concerned about designer labels on our clothing? Do we flaunt our wealth with large houses, new cars, and the latest fashion trends? Are we guilty of judging people by external appearances? Do we enjoy our material possessions too much, or do we focus on love and concern for those who have fewer material possessions than ourselves? The real issue does not concern our self-condemnation of ourselves for the good things that God has provided for us. It is not a question of what we possess, but rather of what we are prepared to give to others.

The anointing from the Holy Spirit is not given for our own convenience or comfort. The Holy Spirit brings us power, not that we might increase ourselves and our possessions, but that we might serve others with the love of Jesus. The anointing that God provides for His servants is so that we might give of our very best for others.

As I stated earlier, William Temple, a former Archbishop of Canterbury in my homeland, announced the great enduring truth that "the church is the only human society that exists for the benefits of its non-members."[5] In other words, we were not meant to tenaciously limp our way toward heaven, barely making it there ourselves, but the Holy Spirit has been given to empower us so that we might change our world for Jesus.

19

A New Day Dawning

ooking down from the platform I could see a miracle happening in the congregation below. Row after row of
Christians were praising God—each one comfortable as they
worshiped in the way that came most naturally to them, but all
choosing to express their worship in different ways from the
others around them.

For so long we have been programmed into doing things the
"right" way. We have been conditioned into doing the same thing
at the same time, and uniformity has become the order of the day.
But on this occasion my eyes strayed along a row to see a glorious
variety of Christians in worship, each accepting the others, differences included! One had his arms straight up in the air, while his
neighbor's hands were firmly at her sides. Next to them stood a
married couple, the husband with his hands outstretched at hip
height and his wife with her hands grasping their song sheet.
Another man had his hands in his pockets, while his wife danced
in the aisle! All were worshiping God in their own way. Some
offered their hearts and lives to the Lord in a quiet meditative
fashion; others expressed their sense of joy and gratitude with
total abandon.

Since that day, I rarely visited a meeting of Christians in the
United Kingdom where such a variety was not demonstrated.
Each person is comfortable in offering to God his own worship

but refuses to be thrust into the straightjacket of copying his neighbors. The miracle lies in the fact that no one dismisses a brother or sister as either being too emotional or too traditional. A quiet spirit of mutual appreciation is beginning to dawn upon us; whether in new or old churches, established or independent denominations, youth or traditional services, we have begun to allow one another to be who we are in Jesus.

The great thing about our variety of church traditions and denominations is that we can choose the one in which we can feel most comfortable. However, we must never do so with an attitude that shows contempt for those who choose to worship in a different way. If a Christian's actions and words conform to scriptural standards, they can and will please God, even if they are different from our *own* normal and accepted form of worship.

COMMUNICATING THE CONCEPT OF WORSHIP

The word *worship* is one of the great words of the church, but unfortunately, it is also one of the most misunderstood. A word regularly used can prove the old adage that "familiarity breeds contempt." For example, the more we talk about Sunday morning worship, the easier it is to define "worship" as the activities that precede the sermon! Now these activities may well be worshipful, but they do not present a complete picture of Christian worship.

The Presbyterians posed one of the key questions of church history when they asked, "What is the chief end of man?" Their own answer was one that is echoed by Scripture and the apostles, prophets, and saints since the world began: "To glorify God and to enjoy Him forever." To worship God is to fulfill the whole purpose of His creation. He created us to worship Him!

Rather than attempt yet another definition of the word *worship*, let us instead look at all the facets of this glorious concept.

Worship involves expressing God's great "worthship."

In the same way that lovers whisper to each other their true feelings, so we worship God when we tell Him how much He is worth to us!

Worship must never be cold or impersonal.

For too long our worship has been confined to a rigid process or ritual. But true worship is felt in the heart. Unimpassioned worship is impossible. To participate in worship means to get involved in honestly expressing to God our love for Him.

Worship is an expression to God of what He is to us!

In some appropriate manner, be it singing, prayer, reading of Scripture, meditation, or some other means, we will express "a humbling but delightful sense of admiring awe and astonished wonder."[1]

True worship only happens when we have stopped trying to stand before God and speak from our own wisdom.

Worship is for those who are humbled and who understand that they are creatures before their Creator. As Jesus said, "I will show you whom you should fear: Fear him who, after the killing of the body, has power to throw you into hell" (Luke 12:5).

Worship incorporates the praise of a grateful people, joyfully acknowledging all that God has given them.

It took the words of a twentieth-century evangelical prophet to help me to realize just how crucial the issue of worship really is. As A. W. Tozer observed:

> Without worship we go about miserable.... The purpose of God in sending His Son to die and rise and live and be at the right hand of God the Father was that He might restore to us the missing jewel, the jewel of worship; that we might come back and learn to do again that which we were created to do in the first place—worship the Lord in the beauty of holiness, to spend our time in awesome wonder and adoration of God, feeling and expressing it, and letting it get into our labors and doing nothing except as an act of worship to Almighty God through His Son, Jesus Christ. I say that the greatest tragedy in the world

149

today is that God has made man in His image and made him to worship Him, made him to play the harp of worship before the face of God day and night, but he has failed God and dropped the harp. It lies voiceless at his feet.[2]

ENJOYING THE PRACTICE OF WORSHIP

How can we as creatures, and sinful ones at that, properly worship our Creator? God Himself has taken the initiative to teach us what to do. When Adam sinned, he didn't go looking for God; God came seeking him. When mankind lost the ability to worship God, the Lord restored that gift through His Holy Spirit: "Be filled with the Spirit. Speak to one another with psalms, hymns and spiritual songs. Sing and make music in your heart to the Lord" (Eph. 5:18–19). One purpose of our being filled with the Spirit is to enable us to encourage each other in our worship of the Lord.

Of course, we can worship God while alone. But true worship is a practice that we develop together, not apart. It is as we support one another that our natural function as creatures worshiping our Creator is reestablished. The Holy Spirit gives us continuous, daily refreshing from God to enable us not just to praise God, but also to encourage that same spirit of worship in each other. The result is that God will be enthroned on the praises of His people. In other words, as God gives us the strength, we give Him the honor and acclaim that is His due.

How are we to worship God?

In corporate worship

Corporate worship involves not just going through the motions of a well-established routine, but also bringing a specific offering from our own hearts to the Lord. It is becoming ever more important for local churches to give the opportunity for members of the body to contribute to acts of corporate worship. The other side of the coin is that worshipers must then be prepared to receive either encouragement and endorsement or gentle guidance and help if they have gone wrong! Such gentle discipline creates an atmosphere of security and support in which each member of the body can deepen their worship of the Lord. Whether it is with a prayer, a song, a reading, a hymn, or a word from the Lord, we all have a contribution to make.

In meditation

Meditation simply involves taking a phrase of Scripture and reflecting upon its truth. For example, we might meditate on the verse, "He who has the Son has life" (1 John 5:12). In this frenetically busy world, it is therapeutic to take time—in the car, at the kitchen sink, during lunch—and allow those words to minister the truth of God's Word to you. Digest them—and worship Him! It is just a phrase of Scripture, but the Holy Spirit can apply it to your spirit to generate genuine worship.

In praise and prayer

The worship of a grateful heart is expressed in thanksgiving to God for all that He has given. Only a few years ago such praise would have been expressed in a very subdued fashion. And quiet gratitude voiced in simple prayer is still the means for many to express their praise. However, other forms of expression have also become the norm in a wide variety of churches. Over the last thirty years a whole new vocabulary of worship has emerged. It uses contemporary styles of music to accompany lyrics that are often based on the words of Scripture, but are less formal than traditional hymns. These provide a genuine means of encouraging one another to praise and thanksgiving.

Other new styles of worship have also acquired new prominence. There has been a rediscovery of the biblical teaching that our bodies can be used in worship. Dance, either in specially choreographed sequences or as a spontaneous expression of praise to God, has opened new dimensions for some, while others have found that the lifting of hands to the Lord is a helpful expression of devotion and gratitude.

Through spiritual gifts

In hundreds of churches, drawn from a variety of different denominations, the use of spiritual gifts has acquired a new prominence. In many churches, the regular use of the gift of tongues with accompanying interpretation, as outlined in 1 Corinthians 14, has become a significant means of stimulating communal worship of God. Prophecy, words of knowledge and encouragement, and other gifts of ministry also have their place in corporate worship. Healing services have become a regular feature in the most unlikely church situations. This same pattern is also witnessed in the worship styles. Even in England, Christians are experiencing a reaction against the years in which traditionally conservative British evangelical Christians were nicknamed "God's frozen chosen"!

AVOIDING THE PITFALLS OF WORSHIP

As with every good thing, there are hazards that we must be careful to avoid. The growth of free expression in worship can easily lead to dangers, which, if not avoided, Satan can use to direct large numbers of God's people into a spiritual cul-de-sac from which they will not easily escape. Some of these pitfalls include:

Overenthusiasm

Recently I found myself sitting on the platform at a meeting while a woman danced gaily up the aisle. A few moments later another followed suit. I turned to my neighbor to check whether or not he felt as I did. One woman was allowing her love for the Lord to be expressed naturally through her dance, while the other looked suspiciously as if she were trying to draw attention to herself. We need to watch our motives and remember Paul's gentle words of censure: "Everything should be done in a fitting and orderly way" (1 Cor. 14:40).

Spiritual superiority

In some churches, spiritual worth is measured by whether or not you speak in tongues, raise your hands, or dance! Such attitudes are dangerously immature.

Paul precedes his instructions to behave correctly with these words: "Therefore, my brothers, be eager to prophesy, and do not forbid speaking in tongues" (1 Cor. 14:39). Yet nowhere in Scripture is there any teaching that those who do not speak in tongues are second-class citizens spiritually!

The purpose of the gift of tongues is to enable us to praise God when we run out of words. We can share with the Lord all that we feel about Him only to discover that we are speechless with wonder, so He simply provides new words to add to our praise.

Many are confused as to how we receive this gift. We should be careful to avoid setting forth any specific methods or techniques—that is unbiblical and can be dangerous. Some years ago I found myself talking to a Christian businessman from a charismatic evangelical church. He longed to praise God in tongues but had never felt free to do so. I pointed out that if he wanted to talk to a non-Christian about Jesus, he would hardly ask the Lord for the words, open his mouth, and sit there awkwardly, gaping open-mouthed at the non-Christian, waiting for words to miraculously come out! He would begin to speak out. So it is with the gift of tongues. We should never make gift of tongues so "supernaturally complicated" that people become afraid of it!

Tongues may be used in public worship. But in this setting, Paul insisted that interpretation must follow; otherwise, "how will anyone know what you are saying? You will just be speaking into the air.... Anyone who speaks in a tongue should pray that he may interpret what he says" (1 Cor. 14:9, 13). Because a tongue is an expression of praise to God, the interpretation will usually similarly reflect the praise of a worshiping heart.

Some of us are quite satisfied with praising God in our own language. Others appropriate the gift of tongues and find that it enables them to better express the devotion of their hearts to the Lord. Paul encouraged the Corinthians to balance praying in the Spirit with praying in the mind. He insisted that both are fruitful, and that the former is not superior to the latter, or vice versa.

Paul expressed his deepest concern when he said, "Since you are eager to have spiritual gifts, try to excel in gifts that build up the church" (1 Cor. 14:12).

Self-centeredness

On the one hand, we can become too immersed in fulfilling our own desires; on the other, we become too concerned with what others are doing. In the latter case we concentrate so much on the actions and attitudes of those around us that we begin to neglect the One who should be the true focus of our worship. The same danger applies to the former case, if things that are good in themselves are carried to an unfortunate extreme. It is possible to overemphasize our freedom in worship to the detriment of other important things.

A friend of mine recently went away on a special weekend retreat where a great deal of time and emphasis was spent on movement and dance. These exercises in "spiritual aerobics" were good in and of themselves, but they took up so much time that no mention was made during the whole weekend of how Christians could minister to their hurting society or be involved in real evangelism.

This is especially true in the area of spiritual gifts. It is possible to place so much emphasis on the Spirit's present-day ministry among us that we do not pay enough attention to His eternal character. If we are not careful, we can find ourselves concentrating too much on our own spiritual excitement rather than on what God wants to do through our lives. We may even be emphasizing the gifts and neglecting the Giver!

It is very easy to become so committed to worship that we become totally self-indulgent. God is after neither our worship nor our service in isolation one from the other. He longs to create a cycle in which, having expressed our love for Him, we then long to share that good news with others. Their response will, in turn, provide further reason for our expression of gratitude to God.

When our emphasis is always on service, we will tend to revert to good deeds out of duty rather than as a free expression of love to God. But when our concerns are confined to only worship meetings, we will tend to add to the already overfull Christian calendar while blindly ignoring a dying world.

Worship
(Sharing our love with God)

Praise
(Sharing our gratitude)

Service
(Sharing that love with others)

Witness
(Sharing the good news)

If our expression of worship to God is to be an acknowledgment of His "worthship," recognizing His position in relation to us, then we must do what He tells us. It is not enough to offer lip service to a living God; He requires actions as well. As the prophet Samuel rebuked a disobedient king, "Does the LORD delight in burnt offerings and sacrifices as much as in obeying the voice of the LORD? To obey is better than sacrifice" (1 Sam. 15:22).

It is not enough to sit on the fence enjoying our own worship. Nor should we spend our time judging the different styles of worship among us. Instead, we must bring to the One who gave everything to us the offering of our lips and our lives. In other words, we must worship God both in what we say and in how we live. Let us spend less of our time examining the worship of others and more of our time asking whether our own worship is acceptable to God.

> So then, my friends, because of God's great mercy to us I appeal to you: Offer yourselves as a living sacrifice to God, dedicated to his service and pleasing to him. This is *the true worship that you should offer.*
> —ROMANS 12:1, GNT, EMPHASIS ADDED

20

RECEIVING THE SPIRIT

What could be easier than receiving the Holy Spirit? Jesus promised His disciples that He would not leave them as orphans, and at the very moment we surrender our lives to Him, He invades our lives with His Holy Spirit. That should be all, shouldn't it?

In a sense, the answer is yes, but another question remains. Why do so many sincere, born-again Christians begin to plead for a deeper experience of God later in their spiritual walk, while others seem to have received all they need at the point of their initial conversion? At this point, evangelical Christians will usually begin to disagree with each other. Differing beliefs about the role of the Holy Spirit in the lives of individual Christians have been the biggest single cause of internal division within the church over the past thirty years.

The epicenter of this controversy is the use of the phrase "baptism with the Holy Spirit." The question is whether or not this baptism refers to a one-time instantaneous experience that occurs at some point after conversion. The second question is whether this is an essential spiritual experience for all believers. And third, is the necessary evidence for this "baptism" that one immediately speak in other tongues?

Receiving the Spirit

A SMORGASBORD OF CHOICES

"He breathed on them and said, 'Receive the Holy Spirit'" (John 20:22). When Jesus commanded something to take place, it certainly happened, and so His disciples definitely received the Holy Spirit at that point. But only a few weeks later, eleven of those disciples were among a crowd of 120 who received a mighty baptism in the Holy Spirit. They then began to speak in other tongues and went out to turn their world upside down!

Is their experience necessary for us today?

Jesus also received an anointing for service at His own baptism. He did not experience a tongue of fire over His head because He had no need to be purged of sin, but what alit on His head was a gentle dove. The Holy Spirit has always been descending like a dove.

One Anglican clergyman friend of mine has received, with a number of fellow clergy, a baptism with tongues of fire. Hundreds of thousands of Christians have received a mighty baptism with the Holy Spirit and then began to speak in other tongues. Yet many of these who have received that gift from God have not turned their world upside down, and many Christians who have no claim to that kind of experience have contributed mightily to the body of Christ and the world in which they live. In Scripture and in the experience of many today, there is often a connection between a special anointing of the Spirit and speaking in tongues, but not every incidence in Scripture or in the experience of many has produced the same connection.

Others have claimed to receive the same kind of baptism in the Holy Spirit, but in much quieter fashion. Drawing comfort from the apostle Paul, who confidently asserted in 1 Corinthians 14:18, "I thank God that I speak in tongues more than all of you," they argue that Paul "grew into the gift" because Scripture does not record that he exercised this gift the same moment when he was filled with the Spirit.

A fourth viewpoint challenges the claim that we need a specific, one-time experience of the Holy Spirit altogether.

157

DESCENDING LIKE A DOVE

Proponents of this view emphasize the need for us to be "sanctified by the Holy Spirit." Although we do not attain to all of God's ultimate standards for our lives at the moment of conversion, we do receive all that we need in order to achieve those standards. Besides which, they point out, our concentration should surely be upon Jesus rather than the Holy Spirit!

FILLED IN DIFFERENT WAYS

The problem is that there is real truth in each one of these arguments. Each viewpoint has had its adherents throughout the history of the church—sometimes few, sometimes many. So at least we are not alone in our confusion! The following list represents the major views that have been suggested about the "baptism in the Holy Spirit":

1. While the Holy Spirit is fully received at the moment of conversion, latent potential within Him is only fully experienced at a subsequent moment of spiritual release.

2. Spiritual regeneration and our baptism with the Holy Spirit coincide with our baptism in water.

3. Our individual conversion is a once-and-for-all-event. This is followed by a gradual work of sanctification (to make us to be more like Jesus), which is initiated and carried out in our individual lives by the Holy Spirit.

4. The baptism seals our lives by the Holy Spirit who brings the assurance of our personal salvation.

5. The baptism of the Holy Spirit is a second experience that takes place after personal conversion. It normally takes the form of a "crisis experience," and it introduces the believer to new dimensions of worship, faith, and the use of spiritual gifts.

158

6. Another view is similar to the last, but it insists on the use of the gift of tongues as the initial evidence that this baptism has been received.

7. The believer is cleansed from all sin by a second work of God's grace in his or her life. Sanctification is not a gradual process of growth, but a direct gift of God. It is given in response to faith and comes as instantly as the tongues of flame at Pentecost.

8. The baptism is an enduement of power that comes to the believer after conversion; it is designed to make the believer more effective in Christian service.

The third view listed here is the one traditionally most associated with "non-charismatic evangelicals." They maintain that every Christian receives all the power he or she needs at the time of conversion. All that is required following the salvation experience is its consistent working out in the life of the believer. Any subsequent "crisis" is simply one of the many close encounters that an individual may have with God during the spiritual journey.

Views five and six represent the Pentecostal and charismatic-evangelical perspectives. Here the emphasis is on the need for Christians to receive a crisis experience in the Holy Spirit sometime after conversion. The baptism in the Holy Spirit will then provide believers with deeper intimacy in their relationship with God, greater potential for victory over ongoing sins in their lives, a stronger sense of personal emotional freedom, more release in worship, and the use of spiritual gifts. This is certainly an extravagant and desirable list of blessings, but it is only fair to point out that the baptism is just the beginning, not the end, of the journey toward their spiritual discovery.

We must never insist that everyone else follow the same spiritual path that God has led us on as individuals. To demand that all others be like us is probably an indication of our personal insecurity rather than divine intention. The living God is perfectly able to lead His people by different routes to the same destination.

The same caution should also apply to our use of terms. In the New Testament, the term "baptism in the Holy Spirit" is often associated with repentance and faith as part of the conversion experience. Since that time, those Christians who have come to a deeper experience of the Spirit after their conversion refer to their experience as "baptism in the Holy Spirit." Because we use these terms in different ways, the danger is that we fail to understand each other.

Interpreting Scripture in the light of our own personal experience can lead to inappropriate feelings of spiritual superiority, as we then assume that we are right and everyone else is wrong. This is a very dangerous practice because it means that we place the power and intentions of God within the narrow box of our own understanding. And instead of allowing others the liberty to find that biblical experience of the Spirit that God has made available for them, we try to lead them into an experience that mimics our own.

Charismatic evangelicals and non-charismatic evangelicals have this in common: they share a heritage that unites them in faith and experience in all areas other than understanding the Person and work of the Holy Spirit. But having seen where we can differ, let us look at how, even on this issue, we have areas of surprisingly broad agreement.

Evangelical Christians all agree that each one of us needs power from God with which to live the Christian life.

In our own human strength we cannot live the life that Jesus asks us to live. The attitudes required and the challenges involved in the Christian life are beyond us. We cannot cope alone.

Our words, actions, prayer, compassion, and witness—all are woefully inadequate. For this reason, the disciples were forbidden to go out as missionaries before the Day of Pentecost (Acts 1:4). The result would have been an overwhelming spiritual disaster. In the same way we need the Holy Spirit to use our lives as containers for Himself. Then our words, actions, prayer, compassion, and witness come from God Himself.

**That power is available to all of God's people—
because each of us receives the Holy Spirit at
conversion as the promise of all that He longs to
achieve in us.**

The fulfillment of our divine potential is often hindered by our
basic weaknesses, so these must be removed by the Holy Spirit
before He can do a full and complete work in us. Self-doubt, insecurity, guilt, anxiety, and sin are always the prime target for His
divine activity. We tend to despise ourselves, but the Holy Spirit
longs to reveal to us the reality that we are God's creation and that
He doesn't create junk! Our feelings of personal inadequacy can
only be removed by His gentle touch.

He longs to cleanse and release us from our failures. At the very
moment we recognize our inability to do the will of God, we surrender to the Holy Spirit the right to replace our feeble human
struggles with a divine power and initiative, which no power on
earth could ever duplicate. When we then realize that by His Spirit
Jesus can achieve all things within us, we discover the glorious
freedom of allowing Him to be God in us!

**We believe that the Holy Spirit wants to achieve more
in our lives than a mere one-time experience could
achieve.**

Paul's words in Ephesians 5:18, "Be filled," are both a command
and an instruction. More literally translated they read, "Continue
to be being filled." In other words, they speak of a daily, ongoing
release of the Holy Spirit in our lives. If we are trying to live today in
the strength of any past experience, be it our conversion or a later
filling of the Spirit, we will only be disappointed.

The famed American evangelist Dwight L. Moody was once
speaking to a nineteenth-century British congregation on this
theme, and some, particularly among leaders and clergy, were
offended by his words. Moody was taken to one side after the
meeting and interrogated. "Why do you say that we need to go on
being filled with the Holy Spirit—we were filled twenty or thirty

years ago! Why do we need to be filled again?"

Moody's reply was a classic of spiritual common sense: "I need to be filled with the Spirit every moment of each day because I leak."[1]

We are still a very leaky people who desperately need to know the reality of God in our experience today—not just in our memories!

A sense of holy dissatisfaction with the poverty of our knowledge of God and our love for Him would quickly transform the situation. No longer would we be content with merely knowing about God; we would hunger to know God, and not just by hearsay! In other words, we would demand a deep, intimate relationship with our Creator. The Holy Spirit Himself prompts that very desire in our hearts.

The Holy Spirit brings more than gifts to the people of God; He produces fruit in our lives.

In Galatians 5:22, Paul spoke of one fruit that has nine flavors: love, joy, peace, patience, kindness, goodness, faithfulness, gentleness, and self-control. These must always lie at the heart of the Christian life.

Every major passage in the New Testament on the subject of gifts is accompanied by a passage on the fruit (Rom. 12; 1 Cor. 12; Eph. 4; 1 Pet. 4). This is because the fruit and gifts are coessentials. The effective exercise of spiritual gifts depends upon the fruit of the Spirit. The Corinthian church tried to use one without the other and became a spiritual disaster. As Peter Wagner says, "Gifts without fruit are like a car tire without air—the ingredients are all there, but they are worthless."[2]

FRUIT-BEARING FOR BEGINNERS

When it comes to the subject of bearing fruit for Jesus in our daily lives, most of us will simply feel like raw beginners. Yet the good news is that we do not have to achieve this on our own. A fruit-filled lifestyle is what the Spirit of God wants to create among the disciples of Jesus. Nor is there one single stereotype to which everyone must conform. We will all still be different, but there will be common characteristics that emerge from the fruit that He brings into our lives.

We will never be able to produce spiritual fruit by our own good resolutions or self-effort. It is a natural process, as fruit-bearing always is. After all, when did you last see an apple tree in the middle of an orchard struggling for breath, writhing in agony, and screaming to produce apples, cores, stems, or leaves? Yet many Christians seem to try to please God by this very kind of process!

What does an apple tree require in order to grow and produce fruit? It needs sunlight, roots, and moisture. When those ingredients are in place, growth becomes a natural process. In the same way, if we are open to the sunlight of God's love, rooted in our relationship with Him through our Bible reading and prayer, and relaxing in the fullness of His Spirit in the Christian community, growth and fruit are inevitable.

The problem for so many of us is that we are still trying too hard! We suffer from our vanity, which demands that we must play a significant part in God's divine activities within our lives. Our insecurity shouts that everyone else must follow the same spiritual pathway that we do. Our fears compel us to strive and go on striving. All of our self-effort will never produce spiritual fruit, because that is the prerogative of the Holy Spirit alone.

Despite all these areas of agreement, the doctrine of the Person and work of the Holy Spirit remains at the center of one of the greatest controversies that the church has faced since its inception. Brother has been set against brother, denominations have divided, churches have split, and in some cases their witness has been destroyed. And individual Christians have limped along seeking one spiritual experience after another.

Argument and debate have proved inconclusive, as A. W. Tozer has put it:

> An enemy has done this. . . . Satan has opposed the doc-
> trine of the Spirit-filled life about as bitterly as any other

doctrine there is. He has confused it, opposed it, surrounded it with false notions and fears. Lies have blocked every effort of the church of Christ to receive from the Father her divine and blood-bought patrimony. The church has tragically neglected this great liberating truth—that there is now for the child of God a full and wonderful and completely satisfying anointing with the Holy Ghost.[3]

FOR THOSE WHO NEED A CRISIS!

The growth of the charismatic or Pentecostal emphasis in the church has proved to be astounding. Chile, Brazil, Colombia, and Korea are just a few examples of this type of spiritual growth. The twentieth century was labeled as "the era of the Holy Spirit," and a new emphasis has been placed on the need to "know God" more fully.

The question is—how?

Faced with that question, many have withdrawn to the safe ground of their own experience of God. Yet time and again Scripture shows God working in a *variety* of ways to answer individual needs. Only one thing is certain, and that is that God wants His people to be filled with His Spirit. How He does it is a matter best left for each of us to determine under His direction rather than our own inclination.

Begin to ask Jesus to fill you with His Holy Spirit. If He assures you in your heart that He has done that already—then keep going! If He does not, then do the following:

- Present yourself (Rom. 12:1–2)
- Ask (Luke 11:9–11)
- Obey (Acts 5:32)
- Have faith (Gal. 3:2)

Don't tell God how He must operate, and don't resist the gifts that He would give you. Don't be afraid to speak in tongues if the Lord encourages you in that direction, but don't condemn yourself if you don't. As someone once said, "The baptism of the Holy Spirit in its final analysis is not manifestations; it is not gifts. The baptism of the Holy Spirit in its final analysis is the revelation of Jesus."

If you still feel uncertain or unclear after taking these steps, don't hesitate to go to a mature Christian, perhaps your pastor, who can help. Remember that Paul had to wait for Ananias to come and lay hands on him, and we may need to receive the laying on of hands as a trigger.

I will never forget that day at four o'clock in the morning. I was conducting an evangelistic campaign at a small church on the south coast of England, yet I knew that I myself needed a touch from God. After the Lord had torn me apart through the witness of a university student on my team, I admitted my need and recognized for the first time that I needed help. I had to acknowledge that I could not get through on my own. I asked that student to pray for me—and he and his girlfriend laid hands on my head and prayed, "Father, I don't even know why we're doing this, but because it was done in Scripture we're following that example. Please empty Clive of himself, and then fill him. Flood his life with Your Holy Spirit."

That morning, over three decades ago, saw the beginning of a whole new chapter in my own spiritual experience. I did not receive all that God had for me in that instant, but an exciting pilgrimage had begun.

You see, each one of us is very like a hotel, full of many different rooms, one for each aspect of our lives. God wants to empty each one of those rooms, clean them out, and move in to inhabit them for Himself. So often we want to limit the areas of our lives in which God is allowed to rule and to reign. We often try to confine the sovereign Lord Himself to just one room—and that will never be sufficient.

God wants us to learn that apart from His Spirit we can achieve nothing. "For what I do is not the good I want to do" (Rom. 7:19). We need to be filled each day with the Holy Spirit so that we may live in God's strength rather than our own. It is not that we will become automatically sinless, but it is in order that we may learn to sin less and less and less!

For too long we have hidden in fear from that simple, but basic and life-transforming work that God wants to do within each one of us. J. I. Brice once pointedly remarked that "the church has halted somewhere between Calvary and Pentecost."[4] I heard another preacher comment that "the average spiritual temperature in the church is so low that when a healthy man comes along, everyone thinks he has a fever."

If we are to see a major move of God in our nation, then that work will begin in individual lives. If we are to challenge our society with the good news of Jesus, we must discover a new power from outside of ourselves. The source of that power lies within God Himself. The Holy Spirit lies at the very heart of our mission. He is the "Helper" whom God has given to us. He is our Guide who not only points out the direction for us to go, but also takes us there.

We must never forget that the One who indwells our lives is no less a Person than the Holy Spirit of the living God. Jesus sternly forbade sinning against His Spirit, and the apostle Paul warned us of the danger of grieving the Holy Spirit. In the Old Testament the Holy Spirit was even sometimes withdrawn from those who had once known His power. Now that Jesus has bequeathed His Spirit to us, we have the guarantee that He will never be removed. But this does not mean that we should ever take the Holy Spirit for granted. We must always be ready and willing to allow Him to move us on.

I can almost imagine Paul raising his index finger as he to admonished the church in Thessalonica: "Do not put out the Spirit's fire" (1 Thess. 5:19). We need to take that same warning to heart today—and let the Spirit's fire burn!

To some of us the call will come simply to humble ourselves and pray; others will need to seek ministry and help. But the end result will be the same—lives filled and renewed by the Spirit of God. Then and only then will people recognize what they saw in those early disciples—the life of Jesus reflected in His people. That is the reason the Holy Spirit has been given, not to point in His own direction, but to draw the attention of everyone toward Jesus. Some years ago I was conducting a mission in a city on Britain's south coast. During the mission, I met a roly-poly, cheerful individual named Charlie. He was a university graduate student and a pillar of the local church, twenty-two years old and quite a mature Christian.

One night Charlie came to see me with tears in his eyes. "Clive," he said. "I want a straight answer to a straight question."

"OK, fire away," I replied.

"In the Bible it says that the non-Christians took note that the early church had been with Jesus. But why do none of my friends seem to see Jesus in me?"

That was a question that only Jesus could answer, so we knelt and prayed together that Jesus would take every part of Charlie's life and fill it with His Holy Spirit. I later heard the rest of the story.

Two days later, as Charlie was working in a laboratory with a Pakistani fellow student, he was asked, "Charlie, what has happened to you since the other day? You're a different kind of Charlie!"

Years later, he still is! But a number of non-Christians have met Jesus because they first saw Him living in Charlie. A generation of "Charlies" is the crying need of the day, but it starts with you—and me—and Jesus! Lives that the Holy Spirit touched and entered at conversion need to be filled by Him if we are to live in God's world God's way so that God's world may begin to recognize His love within the lives of His people.

POSTLUDE

We are only now emerging from a long ice age during which undue emphasis was laid upon objective truth at the expense of subjective experience. Wise leaders should have known that the human heart couldn't exist in a vacuum. If Christians are forbidden to enjoy the wine of the Spirit, they will turn to the wine of the flesh for enjoyment. Our teachers took away our right to be happy in God and the human heart wreaked its terrible vengeance by going on a fleshly binge from which the evangelical church will not soon recover, if indeed it ever does. Christ died for our hearts and the Holy Spirit wants to come and satisfy them.[1]

–A. W. Tozer

Notes

Chapter 2
Without the Spirit

1. Leonard Ravenhill, *Why Revival Tarries* (Minneapolis, Minn.: Bethany House Publishers, 1979).
2. "Strong's Electronic Concordance (KJV)," *PC Study Bible* software program, s.v. "*hagios*." Copyright © 1989, TriStar Publishing. All rights reserved.

Chapter 3
Who Is This Holy Spirit?

1. Thomas Carlyle, as quoted in Rev. John H. Hampsch, C. M. F., "The Open Arms of God,"http://claretiantapeministry .org/teachings/OpenArms.html (accessed November 3, 2003).
2. "Strong's Electronic Concordance (KJV)," *PC Study Bible* software program, s.v. "*hagios*."

Chapter 4
The Living God Is at Work!

1. A. W. Tozer, *The Divine Conquest* (Carlisle, UK: OM Publishing, 1979).
2. A well-known saying of Tertullian, who lived in the midst of persecution. *Encyclopedia.com*, s.v. "Tertullian," http:// www.encyclopedia.com/html/T/Tertulli.asp (accessed October 14, 2003).

Chapter 5
Learning to Live

1. Denys Parsons, *The Best of Shrdlu* (London, UK: Pan Books, 1991).

CHAPTER 6
ENEMY AT WORK

1. C. S. Lewis, *The Screwtape Letters* (New York: Harper Collins, 1942).

CHAPTER 7
TRIAL OF STRENGTH

1. F. B. Meyer, as quoted in Rev. Canon Michael Harper, *Power for the Body of Christ*, chapter 3, "Seeing the Promise," http://www.arma.org/au/harper/chapter3.htm (accessed October 14, 2003).
2. A. W. Tozer, as quoted in "We Have a Confident Faith," *Firelighters Scripture Focus No. 29*, November 2002, http://www.firelighters.org.uk/foryou/bible/scripture_29.html (accessed October 14, 2003).

CHAPTER 8
A WORLD WITHOUT ANSWERS

1. "Psychics Now Greatly Outnumber Priests in France," http://archive.anomalies.net/cni-news/CNI.0405.html (accessed November 3, 2003).
2. Blaise Pascal, *Pensées*, quoted in "Standards & Principles 2," *Standards and Principles: Sayings, Quotes, Aphorisms*, http://www.usewisdom.com/sayings/standards2.html (accessed October 15, 2003).

CHAPTER 9
DANGER—POWERS AT PLAY

1. Walter Wink, *Unmasking the Powers* (n.p.: Fortress Press, 1986).
2. Primal-Indigenous, Adherents.com, http://www.adherents.com/Na/Na_518.html (accessed November 3, 2003).

Notes

CHAPTER 10
THE FIGHT OF OUR LIVES

1. Michael Green, *I Believe in Satan's Downfall* (London, UK: Hodder, 1981).

CHAPTER 11
GIFTED BY GOD

1. Elizabeth O'Connor, *Eighth Day of Creation* (Word Books, 1971), quoted in James VanOosting, "Vocation Education," *America*, vol. 187, no. 1, July 1, 2002, http://americamagazine.org/articles/vanOosting.cfm (accessed October 15, 2003).
2. No further information is available for this quote.
3. C. Peter Wagner, *Your Spiritual Gifts Can Help Your Church Grow* (Ventura, Calif.: Regal Books, 1997).
4. Ibid.

CHAPTER 12
GIFTS THAT SOMETIMES CAUSE A PROBLEM!

1. Irenaus, quoted in Henry Bettenson, *The Early Church Fathers* (Oxford, UK: Oxford University Press, 1956).
2. John Wesley, "Sermon Eighty-nine: The More Excellent Way," Wesley Center Online, Wesley Center for Applied Theology, Northwest Nazarene University, http://wesley.nnu.edu/JohnWesley/sermons/089.htm (accessed October 15, 2003).
3. No further information is available for this quote.

CHAPTER 13
POWER TO BE WITNESSES

1. Ontario Consultants on Religious Tolerance, "Religions of the World: Numbers of Adherents, Growth Rates," updated September 24, 2003, ReligiousTolerance.org, http://www.religioustolerance.org/worldrel.htm (accessed

October 15, 2003).
2. A. W. Tozer, *Of God and Men* (Camp Hill, Penn.: Christian Publications, 1995), 35–37, quoted in "August 1: Evangelism: Spiritually Worthy," *Insight for Leaders from A. W. Tozer*, http://gospelcom.net/lmi/tozer.php3?date=08-01-03 (accessed October 15, 2003).
3. Personal knowledge of author from his work with Evangelical Alliance of the UK.
4. Personal knowledge of author from his work with World Relief.
5. Matthew Henry, *Matthew Henry's Commentary on the Bible* (Peabody, Mass.: Hendrickson Publishers, 1997), s.v. "Zechariah 12:9," quoted in Jonathan Willoughby, "A House of Prayer," Rend the Heavens March Article of the Month, http://www.rendtheheavens.org/AoM_03_March.htm (accessed October 16, 2003).
6. R. A. Torrey, "Why God Used D. L. Moody," quoted in Clive Calver and Eric Delve, *God Can Use You* (Basingstoke, UK: Marshalls, 1983).
7. Martin Luther, quoted in Os Guinness, *Doubt* (Lion, 1976), 32, quoted on Quotations A–D, http:www.geocities.com/mike_mcmillan.geo/quota-d.html (accessed October 16, 2003).
8. Sayings of C. T. Studd, http://www.nathan.co.za/ct_studd.asp (accessed October 16, 2003).

CHAPTER 14
NOT JUST FOR ME!

1. Author's personal conversation in 1999 with Eugen (Geni) Begu, then General Secretary of the Albanian Evangelical Alliance.

CHAPTER 15
THE HOLY SPIRIT AND THE CHURCH

1. Dr. James A. Francis, "Jesus—a Brief Life" (American Baptist Publication Society, published circa 1930), quoted in "'One

Solitary Life' Authorship," Ben's File #007, San Joaquin Valley Information Service, http://www.sjvls.org/sjvis/bens/bf007sl.html (accessed October 17, 2003).

CHAPTER 16
LIVING BY THE SPIRIT

1. Andrew Murray, quoted in Jessie Penn-Lewis, *Soul and Spirit* (Leicester, UK: Overcomer Book room, n.d.), 59, quoted in Brian Onken, "Dangers of the 'Trinity' of Man," Statement DT170, http://www.equip.org/free/DT170.htm (accessed October 17, 2003).

CHAPTER 17
ANOINTED FOR WHAT?

1. Bob Hopkins and Richard White, "Enabling Church Planting," copyright © 1995, CPAS, http://www.acpi.org.uk/Enabling%20Church%20planting.pdf (accessed October 17, 2003).
2. Paul E. Billheimer, *Don't Waste Your Sorrows* (Fort Washington, Penn.: Christian Literature Crusade, 1987).
3. A. W. Tozer, as quoted in "We Have a Confident Faith," *Firelighters Scripture Focus No. 29*, November 2002, http://www.firelighters.org.uk/foryou/bible/scripture_29.html (accessed October 14, 2003).
4. Michael Cassidy, *Bursting the Wineskins* (London, UK: Hodder & Stoughton, 1983).
5. Michael Green, *I Believe in Satan's Downfall* (London, UK: Hodder & Stoughton, 2001).

CHAPTER 18
LOVE ON FIRE!

1. World Relief: Where We Work—Africa, Sudan, "Clive Calver Visits Sudan," http://www.wr.org/where_we_work/africa/sudan/calver_visits.asp (accessed October 17, 2003).

2. Author's personal knowledge from his work with World Relief.
3. Ibid.
4. Martin Luther King Jr., quoted in "Litany for Peace," Peace and Justice Support Network of Mennonite Church USA, http://peacemennolink.org/articles/apr.html (accessed November 3, 2003).
5. Bob Hopkins and Richard White, "Enabling Church Planting," copyright © 1995, CPAS, http://www.acpi.org.uk/Enabling%20Church%20planting.pdf (accessed October 17, 2003).

CHAPTER 19
A NEW DAY DAWNING

1. A. W. Tozer, *Worship: The Missing Jewel of the Evangelical Church* (Camp Hill, Penn.: Christian Publications, 1996), 8–9, quoted in "Excerpts from A. W. Tozer," Messages From the Heart, http://www.heart-talks.com/truth27.html (accessed October 17, 2003).
2. Tozer, *Worship: The Missing Jewel of the Evangelical Church*.

CHAPTER 20
RECEIVING THE SPIRIT

1. Dwight L. Moody, quoted in sermon by Rev. Louis H. Zbindem, "The Apostles' Creed: I Believe in the Holy Spirit," March 3, 2002, http://www.fpconline.org/downloads/sermons/020303%20The%20Apostles'%20Creed-Holy%20Spirit%20LZ.pdf (accessed November 3, 2003).
2. Wagner, *Your Spiritual Gifts Can Help Your Church Grow*.
3. A. W. Tozer, *Gems From Tozer: Selections From the Writings of A. W. Tozer* (Camp Hill, Penn.: Christian Publications, 1979).
4. J. I. Brice, quoted in Rick Joyner, "Can a Nation Be Born Again," quoted in "What Is Revival? A Compilation of

Notes

Articles," prepared by Robert I. Holmes, http://
www.storm-harvest.asn.au/articles/whatisrevival.txt
(accessed November 3, 2003).

POSTLUDE

1. A. W. Tozer, *The Root of the Righteous* (Harrisburg, Pa.:
Christian Publications Inc., 1986).